A God-Balanced Life

Who or What Are You Yoked Up With?

By

James Puckett Sr.

ISBN: 978-1-963949-31-5 (Paperback)

ISBN: 978-1-963949-32-2 (Hardcover)

Printed in the United States of America

Preface

Why write a book on balance? I'm glad you asked. You may have read the title and asked yourself this very question. I'm not sure if I know the real answer myself. But what I can answer is how the thought came about.

In the winter of 2019, I received a phone call from someone very close to me, who lives in a different state. This person asked if I would be interested in doing a teaching series for a group of young people about balance and living a balanced lifestyle. This teaching series would last for six consecutive nights, Monday through Saturday. I humbly agreed.

Knowing I had to do a lot of study and research, I started to prepare for the meetings. I was scheduled to teach the series during the summer of 2020. Then the COVID-19 virus hit us, and as you know, things came to a screeching halt. Everything was locked down, scaled back, or canceled. The meetings got canceled, and to this day, I haven't been approached again to offer those teachings. What I was once excited about was now a thing of the past. But little did I know, God had a ram in the bush.

So now, fast forward to October 2021. I don't recall exactly when, but at some point, the word "balance" popped back up in my spirit. At first, I didn't know what to think. Why was the word "balance" coming to me in this way? After a brief time passed, I remembered the invitation I had received to speak about balance. Why would this subject be coming back to me after all this time? "That's in the past!" I thought.

A few days passed, and I felt inspired to pull out the lessons I had prepared for the teaching. That's when this book idea dropped into my spirit. Well, the rest is history. What I thought was dead, God has brought back to life. I do still hope to teach on this subject one day, even if it's at another location, but God has given me a new hope.

Now, the way I am offering this topic will probably be unfamiliar to you. So, I ask you to remove your traditional way of thinking and allow the Holy Spirit to bring some new revelations into your heart, so that He may allow you to see the Word of God in ways that you may not have before. God's Word has so much to offer those who hunger and thirst after Him. With new revelations come new applications.

Just a word of encouragement here: The very thing you thought was dead, God is resurrecting. Maybe the door to your plans has been closed for some reason or other. Even if God had nothing to do with the door closing, He can open another one that no man can shut. Keep that dream and idea alive in you. It's not over until God says it's over. Hope you enjoy the book.

Contents

Introduction

This book is written directly to Christians, which are those who have made Jesus Christ the Lord and Savior of their life. Nothing in this book suggests that you won't go to Heaven if at times you find yourself a little unsteady in your walk. The *only* qualification for going to Heaven is being born again, so this is not a book about whether you'll make it to Heaven. When you accepted Jesus into your life, your spirit was made perfect and fixed for Heaven. However, from time to time, even Christians find themselves wobbling in their daily walk because of the trouble this world's system brings. The goal is to wobble and not fall, because the balanced way of living is the best way. But if you do happen to fall, then get back up and keep getting up.

Let me say right up front that this book is written to me as well as to other Christians. At times in my Christian walk, I too struggle with balance. But over the years, I have come to learn what is necessary to regain that balance and what is necessary to remain upright when I do get a little off-balance. With that in mind, this book is meant to bring revelation about living life the way Christians are called to live. This book addresses the whole person—not just what you do, who you become on Sundays, or who you are whenever you set foot inside a church. It's about what you do and who you are in your everyday way of living. My goal is to influence the way you view life. The purpose is to get Christians thinking in terms of their entire being. The intent is to have every part of your being operating in agreement with the Word of God.

I believe it would be fair to assume that every Christian has a desire to succeed in life. No one intentionally sets out to fail in his or her walk through life. People, but especially Christians, who are serious about succeeding realize that success does not happen automatically or by chance. They know that it is the fruit of many factors, including making good decisions, concentrated efforts, and perseverance, all of which takes an amazing amount of work on their part. But because of the uncertainty of the world we live in, it's not always possible to anticipate what will happen from day to day. Therefore, it can seem difficult or even impossible to succeed at times. This is why I believe it's extremely important that Christians strive to live their life in a balanced way. Either we are balanced, or we are unbalanced. When you look in the mirror, which person do you see?

The Merriam-Webster Dictionary defines "balance" as "being in a state of balance: having different parts or elements properly or effectively arranged, proportioned, regulated, considered, etc." Just like the definition says, every part of our human body should be properly or effectively arranged, proportioned, regulated, and considered for the Lord's work. I believe that man is made up of three parts: body, soul, and spirit. Man, lives in a physical, fleshly body, he has a soul made up of his mind, will, and emotions, and living inside of him is a spirit. Look at 1 Thessalonians 5:23:

So now, may the God of peace make you His own completely and set you apart from the rest. May your spirit, soul, and body be preserved, kept intact and wholly free from any sort of blame at the coming of our Lord Jesus the Anointed (Voice Translation).

That is what I consider to be the whole man: spirit, soul, and body. If you learn to control your mind, will, and emotions (your soul), then you can control your flesh (the body). Once you control your soul and body, then it's much easier to walk in the spirit. Living a God-balanced life means we control the whole person.

The books of 1 and 2 Thessalonians are letters to the church in Thessalonica from Apostle Paul. In 1 Thessalonians 5, Paul writes a heartfelt, gut-wrenching letter about the return of Jesus and how Christians shouldn't be surprised, overwhelmed, or asleep, but rather watchful and ready for His return. I would call this a letter of last instructions, exhortation, and warning to the church of the Thessalonians. Starting at 1 Thessalonians 5:14, Paul writes:

Now we exhort you, brethren, warn them that are unruly, comfort the feebleminded, support the weak, be patient toward all men. See that none render evil for evil unto any man; but ever follow that which is good, both among yourselves, and to all men. Rejoice evermore. Pray without ceasing. In every thing give thanks: for this is the will of God

3

in Christ Jesus concerning you. Quench not the Spirit. Despise not prophesyings. Prove all things; hold fast that which is good. Abstain from all appearance of evil. And the very God of peace sanctify you wholly; and I pray God your whole spirit and soul and body be preserved blameless unto the coming of our Lord Jesus Christ. Faithful is he that calleth you, who also will do it (1 Thessalonians 5:14-24, KJV).

In these Scriptures, Apostle Paul is instructing the church on how they should be living at the time of the Lord's return. One can really see the pastoring spirit coming out in him. Paul gave his whole self to the people of Thessalonica, and now, he is asking the people to give their whole selves to God. There is no doubt that we are living in the last days. Jesus is closer to coming for His church today than He was yesterday. So, these verses paint a very clear picture of how we ought to be living our lives in the here and now.

When God created the Heavens and earth, He did it by faith. When He brought everything into existence, He did it by saying what He wanted; there was no doubt or wavering in Him. God was not double-minded in His decisions. He said what He wanted, and when He spoke it, it came to be. God was balanced in His thoughts, His decisions, and His speech. He said what He meant, and He meant what He said. God was one hundred percent sure about what He wanted, how He wanted it, and when He wanted it done. There was not an ounce of unbalance in His actions.

You and I are "little gods" placed on earth to do the *will* of the Father. We are made in the image and likeness of God the Father—the creator of Heaven and earth (Genesis 1:27). We are to conduct life's business the same way God did. We are called to live a balanced lifestyle, using the Bible as our example. To live that kind of lifestyle, we must not get yoked to the world's way of doing things. We must live a balanced life according to God's Word.

God has placed value on your life, whether you have made Him Lord and Savior of your life or not. He desires that you live up to that value. What value do you place on your own life? How do you compare your life to that of an unsaved person? God took an appraisal of humanity and placed such value on it that He sent His only begotten Son to die on the Cross as a way of reconciling man back into relationship with Him. I was lost. You were lost. God said, "No, no. You are too valuable to leave in a fallen state." Balancing how we live means weighing the advantages against the disadvantages of every act, because there are consequences to our actions. When we live an unbalanced life, there is a contrast between our way of living and the way God desires us to live.

As we look at the world around us, we witness things that we've never seen or imagined. Most of what's happening is out of our control, so it sometimes seems like we're helpless. The world is in an unbalanced state. The church, as a body, is also unbalanced. People in the world are unbalanced. There is an unbalance in many of our homes. Our children are growing up in an unbalanced society. This country has been taken over by a power that feels uncontrollable, like cancer.

So, we as people of God must get back to the basics of life and the Giver of it—Jesus Christ—who is the Way, the Truth, and the Life. Being balanced is living a spiritual lifestyle, which is found in the Word of God. Look at this Proverb:

> A false balance is abomination to the Lord: but a just weight is his delight. When pride cometh, then cometh shame: but with the lowly is wisdom. The integrity of the upright shall guide them: but the perverseness of transgressors shall destroy them (Proverbs 11:1-3).

If you live by anything other than the Word of God, then you're living by a false balance and are therefore unbalanced.

God is calling on Christians to bring the change that this world so desperately needs. Only Christians who are balanced in their walk with God will be able to stand, maintain their balance, and live like the Bible has instructed them. I am speaking of the stable, equally yoked, reconciled to God, balanced Christians. These are the ones that will bring about the change needed for a move of God.

Chapter I
Balance is Important to God

If you are a parent, you probably can remember the time when your child took his or her first steps. You probably took videos and pictures of those precious moments. You were so proud of your little one because they had to first establish balance to keep from falling and then move forward. Similarly, God is just as proud when we as Christians find and maintain our balance in Him.

In the Old Testament days, when most of society was in its early development, people learned to use weight to measure and exchange goods. A balancing method was used to accurately determine the weight. The balance had a beam, which supported in the middle, and a pan hanging by a cord on both ends. Weights made of stone or metal were placed on either side of the scale, and the item to be weighed hung from a hook in the middle. Weight was added or removed until both sides were equal or balanced. This would determine the weight of the item and ensure it was a balanced weight.

At times, it seems that this world we live in is moving so fast that we can't keep up with the necessary tasks for everyday living. People go from here to there trying to balance everything on their plates. Some do it well, while others struggle with the thought of it. It requires a balance on all parts to get everything done. Anything left unbalanced risks the chance of not getting done.

When we hear the word "balance," we may think about balancing on one foot or balancing an object in our hands. We might even imagine balancing work, family, or relationships. Balancing these things is important because they are part of our everyday life structure. Regardless of whatever image comes to mind when you hear the word "balance," it is something that requires focused concentration.

Whenever I hear the word "balance," my mind immediately goes back to a time in my childhood, when I was around three or four years old. I grew up as a sharecropper's kid in the late 1950s, and cotton was one of the main crop farmers would plant and harvest. My mother would often leave me in the care of my older sister while she worked in the field picking cotton. My sister was only three and half years older than me, about seven years old, but there wasn't a daycare or nanny that my parents could leave us at. So, my sister was the babysitter even though we were both just small children.

Now, the reason this comes to mind so quickly when I hear the word "balance" is because one day, when my sister was babysitting me, she decided to do the unthinkable and tried to weigh me on cotton scales. That sounds funny today, but there was nothing funny about it back then.

During those days, one of the scales farmers used to weigh their produce was called a Cotton Pea Scale weight. Unless you grew up in that era, this is likely an unfamiliar scale to you. It looked like a horizontal, flat iron bar with numbers stamped on the side and a hook hanging from it. It also had a huge, heavy, cone-shaped weight made of iron, which is the "Pea." The Pea was used to balance the bar after a sack full of cotton was placed on the hoop.

Antique hanging cotton/tobacco pea scale.

Antique hanging cotton/tobacco scale with 4 lb. "pea" weight.

Three different sizes of antique Cotton Scale Peas.

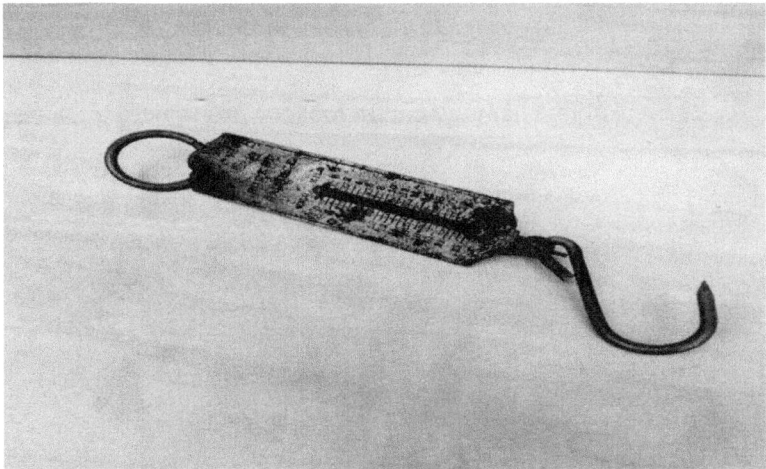

Another type of scale is used to weigh cotton and other harvests.

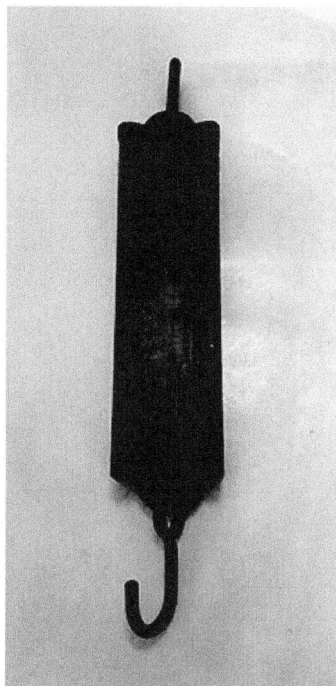

Upright view of a different type of scale for weighing harvests.

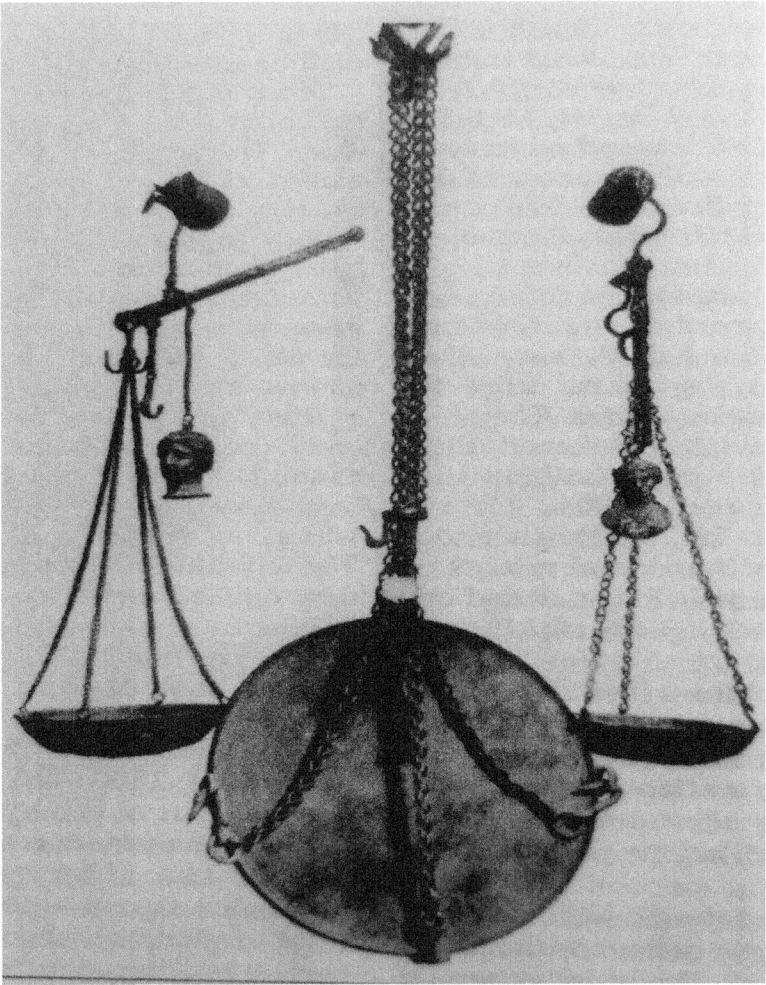

STEELYARDS. These portable balances were designed to be suspended from a hook or from the user's hand. Note the movable weights shaped like the heads of Roman gods. These balances were unearthed at Pompeii; they were buried by the eruption of Mount Vesuvius in A.D. 79.

Source: Nelson's Illustrated Encyclopedia of Bible Facts; J. I. Packer, Merrill C. Tenney, William White, Jr.; page 334, 1995.

So, after placing an empty cotton sack on the scales' hook, she placed me on the cotton sack. She then proceeded to slide the Pea until the bar was balanced out, but she slid it too far. The Pea slid off the bar and landed on my forehead, which caused a good-sized hole. To this day, I have an indentation on my forehead.

That's why, over sixty years later, every time I hear the word "balance," I am immediately taken back to that day. For those who might be wondering, yes, I forgave my sister a long time ago. With that story in mind, you can imagine how important balance can be. When we think about balancing our way of living, it requires careful management and skills. If we choose to live our lives out of balance, then we too are sure to slide off the bar, so to speak. It's equivalent to backsliding from God.

In Proverbs 11, the writer teaches a lot about balance. Specifically, he refers to a balanced lifestyle or a balanced way of living. It's not the example of balance you might think of when you hear that word. The balance he's referring to is a way of living that we should strive for every day. It's choosing to live our lives using the Word of God and allowing it to balance our every move. If we use God's Word like the cotton Pea weight, then we won't have to worry about our lives getting out of balance. Choosing the wrong things or even choosing too much of what seem to be the right things can cause imbalance.

Awhile back, I asked a fellow Christian this question: "When you hear the phrase 'living a balanced lifestyle,' what does that mean to you?" She thought about it for a minute and then gave this answer: "Having everything level in your life." I looked at her and said, "Are you a Christian?" She replied, "Yes!" I said, "So you believe serving the devil as equally as you serve God is balance for a Christian?" She replied, "No," and began to qualify their answer.

I knew what she had meant, but when I heard what she said, it made me analyze it further. The thought occurred to me that her response could be interpreted as: *Christians should give an equal amount of time to the things of the world as they give to the things of God.* She knew this was wrong, and so did I. The point is this: *Balancing our lives for the Lord means thating what He hates and loving what He loves; saying what He has said and rejecting every word that goes against His.*

Imagine the Law of Justice Scale, where something or someone is being judged in the law. The scale could weigh "fairness" on one end and "unfairness" on the other end. The scale would balance out so that there is equal justice on both sides. In this example, balance would mean everyone gets either unequal justice or equal justice. So-called Christians cannot live their lives serving God on this scale of law. God's law goes like this:

> For thou shalt worship no other god: for the Lord, whose name is Jealous, is a jealous God (Exodus 34:14).

14

No man can serve two masters: for either he will hate the one, and love the other; or else he will hold to the one, and despise the other. Ye cannot serve God and mammon (Matthew 6:24).

A false balance is abomination to the Lord: but a just weight is his delight (Proverbs 11:1)

Be ye not unequally yoked together with un-believers: for what fellowship hath right-eousness with unrighteousness? and what communion hath light with darkness? (2 Corinthians 6:14).

Being unequally yoked with unbelievers means separating yourself from them and their unrighteousness and not having any type of fellowship or relationship with them. Likewise, equally yoked would mean that believers should walk in harmony with others of the same faith and belief. Being equally yoked with Jesus means following the teachings of Jesus and keeping His commandments. Christians are to live a life of balance on the Word of God. That's how to live "A God-Balanced Life."

The Scriptures above demonstrate that God is not playing the sharing game. He is not going to share your worship or your money with anything or anyone else. This means we can't have one foot in the church and one foot in the world. Living like this will lead to an unbalanced lifestyle. Money, which will be discussed more in a later chapter, is one area where many Christians are unbalanced. God wants all or nothing. We are to balance our lives by eating at the table God has prepared for us. We don't live by the world's bread, but by every word that God has spoken (Matthew 4:4).

I am not telling anyone what they should or shouldn't eat, but while we're on the subject, it is important to briefly mention balanced eating. We often hear the terms "a balanced meal" or a balanced diet" being tossed around. The world's definition of "a balanced meal" or "a balanced diet" is to eat a variety of foods from all the major food groups. Just like we can't live without physical food, we also can't live without spiritual food. From a spiritual standpoint, it means to eat both physical food and spiritual food. If we eat too much physical food, then we can become sick or even die prematurely. If we eat more physical food than spiritual food, then we will develop a deficiency of spiritual things and become spiritually unbalanced. Likewise, if we only eat spiritual food and not physical food, then we will become weak in our bodies and eventually die. When any of these happen, we are out of balance.

The Bible does say that our body is the temple of the Holy Ghost, and we are told to glorify God with our body (1 Corinthians 6:19-20). So, it *is* important to find that balance with physical food. When it comes to spiritual food, the balance is not based on how *much* you eat, but rather on what you *need* at the time. As spiritual beings, we need spiritual food daily. I will elaborate more on this later. When it comes to spiritual food, which is the Word of God, we are to feast on every word that comes from the mouth of God (Matthew 4:4). The more, the better.

Going back to the story of the scales, imagine your life being a scale, and the scale is balanced by how you should live. Your way of living should be balanced by God's Word. It's very important to look at your life and the way you live in this manner, because any other way of living is unbalanced, making your life a false balance in the eyes of God. This is about a heart balance: the balance of putting God in the place of Lordship in your life and putting yourself in a lesser position. My sister used a false balance to attempt to weigh me that day, and you heard what happened. Don't live your life using false balances. It could scar you for life.

> But seek ye first the kingdom of God, and his
> righteousness, and all these things shall be
> added unto you (Matthew 6:33).

Like the Book of Matthew explains, we are to seek God first. This will keep us in balance with the weight of His teachings. As we discuss the word "balance" in this book, we are talking about living a God-balanced lifestyle by placing our focus on living for Christ, not focusing on ourselves or living like the world. It's vitally important for Christians to stay yoked to Jesus and His teachings. Any other way of living is a false balance and an unjust scale.

Balancing Our Relationships

Remember what 2 Corinthians 6:14 says:

> Be ye not unequally yoked together with un-
> believers: for what fellowship hath righteous-
> ness with unrighteousness? and what comm-
> union hath light with darkness.

Jesus meant it when said that He is the light of the world, and if we believe in Him, we will not walk in darkness (John 8:12). He also said that when we believe in Him, we become that same light (Matthew 5:14).

Now, let's explore the word "yoke." According to the Vines Complete Expository Dictionary, it means serving to couple two things together. It also means submission to authority. There are two important words in this definition: "serve" and "submission." The Noah Webster Dictionary defines "yoke" as: to couple; to join with another of "a pair of scales." Just let those words sink in for a moment: "to couple two things together; to join with another."

Now, let's look at the word "balance." The Noah Webster Dictionary defines it as signifying equal weight or equality; to have on each side equal weight. Both meanings are similar. They both carry the idea of submitting to serve. Before we can faithfully serve one another or in a certain area, we must first learn to submit to that which we are about to serve.

In Old Testament days, large animals called oxen were used to prepare the fields for planting and to thresh out the grain.

They were coupled together by placing a yoke around their necks. To efficiently get the job done, it was vitally important that both oxen were the same height, weight, and strength. If oxen were unequally yoked, they would have a hard time carrying out the tasks required in the field.

This is like people who are unequally yoked. Christians who are not of the same faith or belief cannot collectively do the work of the Lord. They are unbalanced in mind, spirit, and soul. The oxen's yoke symbolizes acts of servitude and carrying the burden for one another for a task or mission. Christians who are unbalanced or unyoked with each other cannot effectively serve each other and have a hard time doing anything for God.

How can people who are not balanced in their beliefs and faith act as burden-bearers? How can believers and unbelievers agree together? How can people who are not yoked with Jesus pray together? These are just a few questions we must ask ourselves as Christians the next time we hear the word "balance" within Christian circles.

When God said, "Thou shalt not plow with an ox and an ass together" (Deuteronomy 22:10), He knew that there would be an unbalance in their shares of the work and that the relationship would not allow for an effective outcome. God knew they would be working against each other because of the imbalance in size and strength. Likewise, Christians are to share the yoke of Christ-like living. We are to live a life of balance using the weight of the Word of God as the scale against which we measure how to live.

Again, when we hear the word "balance," many examples might come to mind. We might think of a person who does a balancing act on a pole while in the water; balancing our step as we walk; a balancing pole used to walk a tightrope. If you are a mathematically-minded person, you might even think of a balanced chemical equation, or some other type of balance. But balance means so much more as it relates to our Christian walk.

When we talk about balancing our relationships, we are referring to allowing those who share a like faith to have a place in our lives and keeping out those who do not share that same faith. This doesn't mean that we don't love people who are of different faiths or beliefs than us. But it does mean that you don't allow them to have a relationship with you. A relationship requires spiritual balance on both sides.

As we see from Proverbs 11:1-3, believers are not to yoke up with people who don't believe as they do. That lifestyle produces unbalanced results. There can be no union or unified relationship with people who do not believe alike, think alike, and act alike as it relates to the things of God. Let us look at 2 Corinthians 6:14 from another translation:

> Do not be mismated with unbelievers. For what partnership have righteousness and iniquity? Or what fellowship has light with darkness? (2 Corinthians 6:14, Revision Standard Version).

The above translation uses the word "mismatched." We all know what it means to mismatch something. We would look silly wearing mismatched shoes or clothes. Of course, wearing mismatched shoes or clothes would probably not hurt us. But from a human standpoint, what if we had mismatched legs, one long and one short? That would affect your whole life in a negative way. You would not be able to function properly. Similarly, to be mismatched or yoked up with the wrong person is not a balanced match and could have negative consequences for your life.

First and foremost, Christians are to be yoked up with Jesus. He commanded us to take His yoke, to walk alongside Him, and to model ourselves after Him. Jesus' yoke is easy because He has designed it that way. Any other yoke is hard and will not last (Matthew 11:29-30). Jesus' desire is that we be "yoked" with Him in our everyday living. Jesus has submitted Himself to serve us in making our hard times easy. This is the "balance" that God intended for His human creation to live by. Anything outside of this type of "yoke" is a false balance and is an abomination to the Lord. If you are not yoked with Jesus, you are living a unbalanced lifestyle.

I already mentioned that I grew up on a farm and that my parents were sharecroppers. We had what you would call "working horses." These horses were used to cultivate the fields at planting time and for other work that needed to be done on the farm. Depending on the nature of the work, only one horse might be used. But when the work was much larger, two horses were used by yoking them together. When preparing horses for plowing, it's important that it's done right. There are several items used to get the horses ready, such as the collar, harness, bridle, and cross lines. Harnessing one horse is easy. But when to comes to harnessing two horses, it gets a little trickier and must be done carefully to ensure each horse has an equal workload.

To tie or connect two horses together, a harness is placed on each of the horses' backs, and then a line from the harness, known as a crossline, is used to hook one horse's bridle to the other. Without hooking them together, each horse would want to go in his own direction, and the handler would not have control of them. Just like God said not to yoke an ox and an ass together, you wouldn't crossline a working horse and a riding horse. They would be unequally yoked and unbalanced. Both are horses, but one is designed to work while the other one is designed to ride. There must be a work-like relationship between both horses. Both horses must have the same work ethic and pulling power. This is like Christians' relationship with other Christians and with God. We must think like God thinks and do like God does. Any other way of living is unbalanced to God.

Balancing Our Relationship with God

Let us look at an example of balance. We live in a time where electronics are the dominant way of doing business. Most money transactions today are done electronically using debit cards or credit cards, but some people still use checks to make transactions or pay bills. I'm sure we've all probably heard the term, "balancing a checkbook." Using the word "balance" in the context of a checkbook can also translate as "reconcile." To balance a checkbook is to reconcile your account. Doing this ensures that your record of how much money you have available matches the bank's record. Your records can't show one dollar amount while the bank's records show another. They must match. If there is a mismatch, then they are not balanced.

The word "reconcile" deserves to be explored a little further. From the Noah Webster 1828 American Dictionary of The English Language, it means to call back into union; to call back into union and friendship the affections which have been alienated. Another definition is: to cause to coexist in harmony; make or show to be compatible. Looking closely at these meanings of the word "reconcile," you can see the correlation between the words, "balance" and "reconcile."

When we balance our way of living to match the Word of God, we are literally reconciling with God. We are forming a relationship with the Father that is compatible with the relationship He had with His Son, Jesus. We are bringing ourselves into order for proper union with our Heavenly Father. To reconcile our lives with the Father is to coexist with and be in harmony with everything He has said. This is balance. Remember, God hates a false balance. God hates it when we are not in a relationship with Him.

Again, remember what Moses said, "Thou shalt not plow with an ox and an ass together" (Deuteronomy 22:10). How can you have a relationship with the God of Heaven and a relationship with the devil at the same time? It's impossible.

23

The ox and the ass will not cooperate with each other. They're incompatible. Likewise, God and the devil are not going to cooperate with each other. The devil has one mission, which is to steal, and kill, and destroy our lives, whereas Jesus' mission is to give us abundant life (John 10:10).

Just as God knew that the ox and the ass would not make a good match in the planting fields, it follows that the same goes for balanced and unbalanced Christians in God's field. Look again and notice how 2 Corinthians 6:14 is worded:

> Be ye not unequally yoked together with unbelievers: for what fellowship hath righteousness with unrighteousness? and what communion hath light with darkness?

God is saying a believer, and an unbeliever cannot have a spirit-like fellowship or relationship with one another because one operates in the light and the other operates in the dark. If you are in a dark room and you want it to remain dark, you wouldn't turn on a light. Why? Because the light would cancel the darkness. Likewise, if you were in a room where there was light and you wanted it to remain lighted, you wouldn't turn off the light. Why? Because light will overpower the dark, and the room will light up. The point is: Light and darkness are like water and oil. They are mismatched; they don't go together; they don't mix well. Never have, never will.

Look how this translation of 2 Corinthians 6:14 says it:

24

Do not be mismatched with unbelievers; for
what do righteousness and lawlessness share
together, or what does light have in common
with darkness? (2 Corinthians 6:14, NASB).

We often go to this verse to address the subject of marriage
relationships. And in its context, that's correct. But this
verse carries the same application as Deuteronomy 22:10.
How can you have a relationship, especially a spiritual one,
with someone who doesn't agree with you about spiritual
things (Amos 3:3)? God said not to mismatch with
unbelievers. The word "mismatch" carries the meaning of
conflict or discord.

Have you ever tried to work with someone on a project or
complete a task and the two of you had different plans or
different opinions for completing it? One of you wants to do
it one way, and the other wants to do it another way. When
this happens, it creates conflict and strife between the two.
The two of you could have a hard time agreeing with each
other about anything moving forward.

Now, I'm not suggesting that we all should think alike or
see things the same, but wouldn't it be nice if people could
at least see and acknowledge the other's point of view and
talk to resolve their differences? Plus, life would be boring
if we all agreed on everything. People of the light and people
of the dark will never see eye-to-eye on spiritual things.
Christians who are out of balance with one another have a
hard time "agreeing to disagree." It just won't happen until
both are balanced by the weight of the Word of God.

25

God has placed us, His people, on His battlefield to plow up the fallow ground and make ready for the harvest (Hosea. 10:12). It's important that believers work together to accomplish His desire. God did not say establish a union with just anyone. He made it clear that fruit can't be produced when believers and unbelievers, righteousness and unrighteousness, light and darkness are yoked together. The balance must be the God kind of balance. A false balance and a just balance are mismatched, and so God hates it.

Jesus told Christians that there is power in agreement. Matthew 18:19 says:

> Again I say unto you, That if two of you shall agree on earth as touching any thing that they shall ask, it shall be done for them of my Father which is in heaven.

Jesus said this to Christians; it came from one Christian to other Christians. This verse will not work if one of the two is a believer and the other one is an unbeliever. This would be an unbalanced approach to Scripture and would be a misjudgment of God on our part. Both people must be yoked together in their belief and faith in God. Any other way is a false balance and is an abomination to the Lord.

Chapter II
Balancing Good Over Evil

If you haven't noticed yet, I want to make you aware that we live in a confusing world. The only thing I can trust is God's Word. The Word of God is the only sound doctrine a believer can follow. Any other doctrines are false and could lead you to become unbalanced, unequally yoked, or unstable in your walk with God. The things that are being forced on Christians are unbelievable. I never thought I would see days like the ones we are living in. The Word of God is, without question, our last and only defense. When we speak Scripture, the devil trembles, the heavens shake, and God answers.

Every day, you and I are faced with and required to challenge false balances. These false balances try to invade our way of thinking and influence our beliefs. They set a false narrative about how we are to live in the sight of God. The debates are nonstop. We find ourselves balancing what is true versus what is false, the case *for* versus the case *against*, Black versus White, Black Lives Matter versus All Lives Matter, God's plan versus the devil's plan, the vaccinated versus the unvaccinated, masks versus no masks, gender identity versus birth gender. The debates are endless.

Christians shouldn't have to debate what's right and what's wrong. We have a book called the Bible that gives us the answers to all our questions. Balancing *good* over *evil* and *right* versus *wrong* can be clearly understood from the Word of God. If it's good, it's from God. If it's bad, it's not from God. Case closed. James explains, "Every good gift and every perfect gift is from above, and cometh down from the Father of lights, with whom is no variableness, neither shadow of turning" (James 1:17).

God was not confused when He inspired James to pen those words. So why are there such debates, especially among the church? Unequally yoked people, people in darkness, unrighteous people, people with untamed tongues, unbelievers, and people living with false balances all contribute to the confusion and division that we face in the world today.

God called His people to be warriors. He has not only created us to have victory in life, but He has also provided us with the equipment to fight off everything the enemy confronts us with (Luke 10:19). I truly believe that. He has also commanded us to dress appropriately for battle. I am reminded of the story in 2 Chronicles about a king named Jehoshaphat.

> It came to pass after this also, that the children of Moab, and the children of Ammon, and with them other beside the Ammonites, came against Jehoshaphat to battle. Then there came some that told Jehoshaphat, saying, There cometh a great multitude against thee from beyond the sea on this side Syria; and, behold, they be in Hazazontamar, which is Engedi. And Jeho-

28

shaphat feared, and set himself to seek the Lord, and proclaimed a fast throughout all Judah (2 Chronicles 20:1-3).

This is the king of Judah, and he was about to face multiple armies. The Bible says this king, who was a warrior, feared. What he does next is what matters: *And Jehoshaphat feared, and set himself to seek the Lord, and proclaimed a fast throughout all Judah* (2 Chronicles 20:3). Notice that he didn't allow fear of the armies to paralyze him or to set him running. Instead, he sought the Lord and proclaimed a fast. He quickly realized where his help would come from. If he was to defeat the armies that were coming against him and his people, then he had to look beyond the evil they were facing and look at what was good and perfect. He thought of the Lord's goodness and asked for His help. He called a fast, assembled the people, and they prayed to the one God, the one good God, that would save them. The story continues:

And Judah gathered themselves together, to ask help of the Lord: even out of all the cities of Judah they came to seek the Lord. And Jehoshaphat stood in the congregation of Judah and Jerusalem, in the house of the Lord, before the new court, and said, O Lord God of our fathers, art not thou God in heaven? and rulest not thou over all the kingdoms of the heathen? and in thine hand is there not power and might, so that none is able to withstand thee? Art not thou our God,

29

who didst drive out the inhabitants of this land before thy people Israel, and gavest it to the seed of Abraham thy friend for ever? And they dwelt therein, and have built thee a sanctuary therein for thy name, saying, If, when evil cometh upon us, as the sword, judgment, or pestilence, or famine, we stand before this house, and in thy presence, (for thy name is in this house,) and cry unto thee in our affliction, then thou wilt hear and help. And now, behold, the children of Ammon and Moab and mount Seir, whom thou wouldest not let Israel invade, when they came out of the land of Egypt, but they turned from them, and destroyed them not; Behold, I say, how they reward us, to come to cast us out of thy possession, which thou hast given us to inherit. O our God, wilt thou not judge them? for we have no might against this great company that cometh against us; neither know we what to do: but our eyes are upon thee (2 Chronicles 20:4-12).

As Jehoshaphat and the people of Judah stood together before the presence of the Lord, He spoke to them. It's obvious that Jehoshaphat was in fellowship with the Lord. He knew that they alone didn't stand a chance against the armies of the enemy. I like what he told the Lord: *Neither know we what to do: but our eyes are upon thee.* What a confession to make when he and the city of Judah were about to be overrun by evil people. Sometimes we just need to just tell God that we don't know what to do. Jehoshaphat knew the only place he could look for help was to the Lord. He knew that no man was going to save them. This is how we must fight our battles of life as well. When evil comes against us, we must seek the Lord for His help. We must admit that we cannot do it on our own and instead seek God. He is willing and able. After Jehoshaphat and the people were finished seeking the Lord, He spoke:

> And he said, Hearken ye, all Judah, and ye inhabitants of Jerusalem, and thou king Jehoshaphat, Thus saith the Lord unto you, Be not afraid nor dismayed by reason of this great multitude; for the battle is not yours, but God's. To morrow go ye down against them: behold, they come up by the cliff of Ziz; and ye shall find them at the end of the brook, before the wilderness of Jeruel. Ye shall not need to fight in this battle: set yourselves, stand ye still, and see the salvation of the Lord with you, O Judah and Jerusalem: fear not, nor be dismayed; to morrow go out against them: for the Lord will be with you (2 Chronicles 20:15-17).

Jehoshaphat did all the right things but notice what he did *not* do. He did *not* complain or seek advice from anyone but God. Jehoshaphat was facing a major problem. The dilemma that he and the people were about to encounter was a matter of life and death. He knew that he and the people were no match for the armies heading their way. Nevertheless, he understood that if he was going to win the fight, he had to invite God to join the battle. He was stable and balanced. He understood that he had to call out to the One who could and would fight his battle—the God of Heaven.

Jehoshaphat didn't waver in his stand against evil; even when he knew he was outnumbered, he and the people stood strong. He didn't hesitate in his decision to call out to God. He confronted the thing he feared by placing his trust in the Lord. He looked evil dead in the eyes and defeated it by calling on his One sure help—the Lord Almighty—the One who will fight your battle when you face evil. Jehoshaphat was yoked with the Lord. He knew exactly what to do, and he was confident that the Lord would do it. There was no unbalance found in Jehoshaphat.

Balance in Our Speech

Jesus desires for us to be "yoked" with Him in our everyday way of living. This is the "balance" that God intended for His human creation to live by. Anything outside of this type of "yoke" is a false balance and is an abomination to the Lord. When we give our lives to the service of Jesus, we are to allow Him to steady our lives in the areas where it is unbalanced.

Let us discuss the tongue for a moment—that small thing inside your mouth. The tongue is, by far, the most powerful and most deadly destroyer of humans known to man. It is more deadly than a deranged person with a loaded gun randomly firing at people. It is more destructive than a fatal disease. The tongue is a small and living instrument that, if left untamed, will expose the deceitful heart of every human being. The bigger problem is that every person has one.

Have you ever been around someone for whom it seems like every other word that comes out of their mouth is unfruitful, negative, evil, or destructive? I certainly have. I used to be one of those people, but one day, Jesus got hold of me and began to tame my tongue. Did it happen overnight? No; to tell you the truth, it was several years later. I really got serious after my salvation, and the desire to say evil, destructive words gradually began to depart from my lifestyle. The old man was diminishing, and a new man was starting to come to life right before my very eyes (2 Corinthians 5:17). You see, I couldn't do it on my own, as much as I tried to. I didn't have the balance of the Word of God in my heart that was necessary for the change. However, no real recognizable change took place until I received the baptism of the Holy Spirit. He made all the difference. Only God can tame your tongue. James says it this way:

> My brethren, be not many masters, knowing that we shall receive the greater condemnation. For in many things we offend all. If any man offend not in word, the same is a perfect man, and able also to bridle the whole body. Behold, we put bits in the horses'

mouths, that they may obey us; and we turn about their whole body. Behold also the ships, which though they be so great, and are driven of fierce winds, yet are they turned about with a very small helm, whithersoever the governor listeth. Even so the tongue is a little member, and boasteth great things. Behold, how great a matter a little fire kindleth! And the tongue is a fire, a world of iniquity: so is the tongue among our members, that it defileth the whole body, and setteth on fire the course of nature; and it is set on fire of hell. For every kind of beasts, and of birds, and of serpents, and of things in the sea, is tamed, and hath been tamed of mankind: But the tongue can no man tame; it is an unruly evil, full of deadly poison (James 3:1-8).

Simply put, by speaking the Word of God, your tongue can cause your life to be balanced, and you will begin to walk in harmony with the Father. But on the other hand, by speaking ungodly and unrighteous words, your tongue will make your life unbalanced. Remember the Pea, which is used to balance the rod of the scale? Earlier, we discussed how it was placed too far to the edge and slid off, damaging my forehead. Your tongue is the same way. When your tongue goes off-script from the teaching of the Bible, it has a language and vocabulary of its own that is spoken from a false balance. Remember what Moses said: *Thou shalt not plow with an ox and an ass together* (Deuteronomy 22:10). To be in balance with God, your tongue cannot speak good sometimes and speak evil other times. When this happens, your tongue is unbalanced and needs to be tamed by the weight of God's Word.

> Out of the same mouth proceedeth blessing and cursing. My brethren, these things ought not so to be. Doth a fountain send forth at the same place sweet water and bitter? Can the fig tree, my brethren, bear olive berries? either a vine, figs? so can no fountain both yield salt water and fresh (James 3:10-12).

Before I was filled with the Holy Spirit, with the evidence of speaking in other tongues, my tongue was a fountain bringing forth both good and evil words, but mostly evil. My tongue was speaking both life and death, but mostly death.

I told you about the time I posed this question to a Christian friend: "When you hear the phrase 'living a balanced lifestyle,' what does that means to you?" He replied, "Having everything level in your life." In the context of the tongue, one would think that means speaking both righteous and evil, both blessings and curses. But this is far from the truth. If we use our tongue this way, then we are unbalanced in our speech and behavior. To be balanced in our speech, we must consistently allow the weight of the Word of God to tame our tongue so that we talk like God talks.

The tongue has a way of setting things on fire where there was never any fuel to begin with. You ask, "If the tongue is so bad, then why did God make it that way?" Let me be clear in my answer. God did not design our tongue to operate in this way. When evil and unrighteous words are produced by the tongue, they are produced from an untamed tongue. God created your tongue to speak blessings, not curses, over your life situations. When we fail to weigh our way of living by the Word of God, we become unbalanced in our talk and sadly, in our walk as well. When this happens, we are dealing with a false balance that is an abomination to God. God delights in a just weight (Proverbs 11:1).

The tongue is an untamable, uncontrollable, poison-filled, deadly weapon that is corrupted by the human heart. It fires shots upon its targets with laser-like accuracy and causes shame, harm, hurt, destruction, and in many cases, death (James 3:8). The Bible says our tongue is the pen of a ready writer (Psalm 45:1). It can either bless or curse (James 3:9). How would you describe your tongue? What stories are you writing about yourself and others with your tongue?

Balance In Our Ways

Remember what we read in Deuteronomy 25:13-16. Moses warned the people about using false balances against their neighbor. Also remember that in Proverbs 11, God warns His children about living in a way that "yokes" them with the world's way of living. Solomon provides proverbs like that to demonstrate the benefits of living a balanced lifestyle versus the disadvantages of living with false balances and unjust weights.

Do you know someone who will not stick to what they say? They consistently change their mind, even when the circumstances surrounding the situation haven't changed. I realize there are times when we can have a change of mind due to changed conditions. So, a change of mind is undoubtedly not out of the question. But changing our minds for no apparent reason displays unbalance in our ways. God had some strong words to say about people like this. In the book of James, God tells us what He thinks about people who cannot be balanced in making decisions and sticking to them. Look at James:

> If any of you lack wisdom, let him ask of God, that giveth to all men liberally, and upbraideth not; and it shall be given him. But let him ask in faith, nothing wavering. For he that wavereth is like a wave of the sea driven with the wind and tossed. For let not that man think that he shall receive anything of the Lord. A double-minded man is unstable in all his ways (James 1:5-8).

Asking God for wisdom is the context of the above verses. When we go to God to gain wisdom about something, He promises that He will give it to us without questions. But He also warns us that we must come to Him with a decided mind and not be unstable or unbalanced in our asking. God does not like when a person cannot make up his mind and is constantly changing it. When we go to God and ask Him for something, that needs to be our final decision.

The word "stable" simply means not likely to give away or overturn; firmly fixed. To be in a stable position is to keep or put (something) in a steady position so that it does not fall. This is how Christians must live their lives. Stability will keep us balanced so we will not fall. A better expression would be stability will keep us from staying down if we fall. I like these verses in Proverbs:

> Trust in the Lord with all thine heart; and
> lean not unto thine own understanding. In all
> thy ways acknowledge him, and he shall
> direct thy paths (Proverbs 3:5-6).

Part of trusting God is seeking Him for understanding in all that we do. He promises to direct us in our ways and on our path. It is very comforting to know that as I go through life in the way of Scripture, He is going to direct my every step.

Do you remember when you first learned to ride a bike? Some of us started out on a tricycle. Learning to ride a tricycle was easy compared to riding a bicycle. Why? Because a tricycle has three wheels and does not require the balance that a bicycle does. I remember when I first ventured out to learn to ride a bike. Learning to ride a bike can be very difficult for some people because balance is required to keep the person from falling and to keep the bike upright. The balance is controlled by the person on the bike. If the person is off-balance, then the bike becomes off-balance too and will fall over. Keeping a bike in a steady roll is a learned skill that must be continued during peddling to keep the rider balanced and prevent the bike from falling over. Both the rider and the bike must always be balanced while riding.

This is why it is important to make Jesus the Lord and Savior of our lives while we are of a young age. Just like it's better to learn the skills needed to ride a bike while one is young, it's better to learn about a God-balanced life at a young age. Learning what it takes to obtain and maintain a God-balanced life at an early age makes it much easier to regain our balance when we see ourselves becoming unstable in our walk with God. As we walk through life, we must maintain our balance in the Word of God to keep us upright and not fall.

1 Corinthians 15:58 says, "Therefore, my beloved brethren, be ye stedfast, unmoveable, always abounding in the work of the Lord, forasmuch as ye know that your labour is not in vain in the Lord." Just as God said, if we are not only unmovable but also steadfast in Him, our labor will not go unnoticed; it's the same as riding the bike. To ride the bike, you must be on the bike, steady in your peddling, and you and the bike will stay upright. Think about the Word of God in that way. If we are balanced in God's Word, do not question any part of it, and do what it says to do, we will stay upright.

Look at James 1:8 from another translation: "[For] Such doubters are thinking two different things at the same time [double-minded], and they cannot decide about anything they do [are unstable in all they do]. They should not think [expect] they will receive anything from the Lord" (James 1:8, Expanded Bible). Double-minded people are unbalanced in all their ways. They have a difficult time deciding on something as simple as what they're going to eat. You might say, "Sometimes I have trouble making up my mind about what I'm going to eat too." Well, so do I. I'm talking about those people who have a hard time deciding and then still end up eating something or somewhere that they don't like. Instead of making a firm decision, they end up settling for something they don't even like.

When James uses the words "double-minded," he is referring to people with two minds. They cannot decide on one thing because they are dealing with two minds—double-minded. One mind is concentrating on one thing, and the other mind is concentrating on a totally different thing. This is a person with two souls, who doesn't have a heart for God. For the most part, people who are unbalanced in their ways are people who have no clue where they're heading in life because they're too busy changing their minds. They can't decide on whether to go to the left or to the right. They look for someone else to choose their way.

Jesus gave us the solution in choosing our way. Jesus said, "I am the way, the truth, and the life: no man cometh unto the Father, but by me" (John 14:6). This is how we are to live. We are to live the way of Jesus, which means being balanced in His way, His truth, and His life. Psalms 128:1 says, "Blessed is every one that feareth the LORD; that walketh in his ways."

Chapter III
Balancing Our Everyday Walk

Balancing how we walk is equally important as balancing how we talk. Every day we should strive to walk in harmony with the Father and His Word. Just as God commanded Christians to be balanced in their everyday walk with Him, He also commands us to behave according to the teaching of Jesus. No one is perfect, but we should habitually seek to pattern our walk and actions after Him. Don't choose to walk through life unbalanced. God loves a just weight in our walk and actions.

Remember, we are talking about living a God-balanced lifestyle. Let's look at the word "balance" from another point of view. This is not a mental or educational balance, but rather a heart balance. Putting God in the position of Lordship in your life and putting yourself in a lesser position is having heart balance. I like to think of it this way: God first, then family, then country, and then work. If we put God first and trust Him, He will help us take care of the rest.

Christians should feast on every single Word of God if they want to have a balanced "diet" and live a God-balanced life. Every Word of God is necessary for living a balanced lifestyle that is pleasing to God. If we pick and choose what words we feed on, we will eventually find ourselves in lack and insufficiency in our spiritual lives, just like we can experience lack and insufficiency of vitamins and minerals in our physical bodies. Look at these verses:

And that from a child thou hast known the holy scriptures, which are able to make thee wise unto salvation through faith which is in Christ Jesus. All scripture is given by inspiration of God, and is profitable for doctrine, for reproof, for correction, for instruction in righteousness: That the man of God may be perfect, thoroughly furnished unto all good works (2 Timothy 3:15-17).

Clearly, to get and maintain a balanced lifestyle in our everyday way of living requires us to feed on the whole Bible. Anything less is an unbalanced and an unjust way of living.

Noah is another one of those Old Testament heroes that we don't read much about. He is known as the man God used to build an ark. As children, all of us probably had this story told or read to us at some point. But there is a detail in the story of Noah that we may never have realized. God didn't just use Noah to build an ark so that he and his family could be saved; God used Noah to save all of humanity. The ark was the tool God used. I imagine God could have used other means rather than the ark, but He didn't.

After God saw that the evil of man was out of control, He was sorry He had created man and vowed to destroy the entire race. He committed to destroying every living creature on the earth, not just man. Even though the land was filled with much sin and evil, Noah kept himself free from everyday violence and corruption. He alone was

43

balanced in the sight of God. The Bible says in Genesis 6:8 that Noah was different, and God liked what He saw. What a novel idea! To be different in the eyes of God. When God looks at you and me, does He see us differently from what He sees in the world?

God was pleased that out of all human creation, He found one man, Noah, who was different from the rest. God was so pleased with Noah's behavior and his relationship with Him that He hand-picked him from amongst all the other men to carry out His *will* upon the earth. What I like about Noah is that he did not have to rehearse for the role he was about to play in God's show of power. This was a part that Noah had been practicing all his life because he kept himself reconciled to the things that pleased God. He was never out of step with God. He kept himself balanced with the *will* of God for his life. The Bible says that Noah walked with God (Genesis 6:9).

Because Noah was not yoked with the rest of mankind's behavior and corruption, and because he stayed steadfast in his faith and beliefs, God chose him over any other man. It's imperative that we keep ourselves balanced in the ways of God in our everyday walk. We must walk with God just as Noah did. Walking with God every day is part of living a God-balanced life.

Micah is another book in the Bible that most people probably don't find themselves reading much—at least I don't. But I do find the book by Micah to be a very intriguing read, and I would like to share a portion of it with you. Micah also has something to say about walking with God. In the sixth chapter, Micah is prophesying to the people and telling them that God is not pleased with their behavior. He reminds them how the Lord brought them out of Egypt and set them free from their slavery and saved them from all the trouble they faced. God tells Micah that He is not asking for any type of offering; all He desires is for the people to do what is just, have mercy towards others, and walk humbly before Him. Let's look:

> Will the Lord be pleased with thousands of rams, or with ten thousands of rivers of oil? shall I give my firstborn for my transgression, the fruit of my body for the sin of my soul? He hath shewed thee, O man, what is good; and what doth the Lord require of thee, but to do justly, and to love mercy, and to walk humbly with thy God (Micah 6:7-8).

God was not concerned about what they had or what they could offer Him. All He wanted was for the people to treat others justly, show mercy, and walk with Him. God knew that if the people would focus on balancing their relationship with Him by humbly walking in His ways, then all the other things would come as a result.

The same is true today. All God wants us to do is stay reconciled with Him by living according to His Word. The Bible says that Job was perfect, upright, feared God, and persistently avoided all evil (Job 1:1). That's the same way that God wants you and me to live.

Noah Believed God

I doubt God would ever tell you or me to build an ark, but He might. Would you believe Him if He did? I wonder what Noah's first reaction was. What did he think? Did Noah say something like "That can't be God! I must be hearing things! That's impossible, God! I'm just one man! I can't do that all by myself!"? The Bible says that after God revealed His plan to destroy the world to Noah, and how He was going to use him in it, that Noah believed God (Genesis 6:22) and did as He instructed him. Noah did not waver from what God had told him. We probably would have responded a little differently than Noah did.

Because Noah walked with God in his everyday life, he had all the confidence he needed. Noah already knew God, he trusted God, and he depended on God. He believed God so strongly that he worked on the ark for 120 years. During those 120 years, Noah continued to preach the Word of God without any doubt whatsoever that what he was doing was the *will* of God. (2 Peter 2:5). Scripture would also indicate that no other man was converted or came to know God during those 120 years, other than his immediate family (1 Peter 3:20). But that didn't stop Noah from building the ark and preaching the Word.

Imagine God waiting 120 years for you or me to give our lives to Jesus Christ. What a long-suffering and merciful

God we serve. The more Noah warned the people, the more they sinned. They continued with their ways until the day of the flood. If you are reading this and you haven't made Jesus Christ your Lord and Savior, I urge you to do it now. Right this minute. God made us a promise that the next time He destroys the world, it will not be by water but by fire. God's hands will bring another day of destruction. Will you be able to escape it? If you're not sure, you can be sure right this minute. Pray this prayer:

> Dear Heavenly Father, I come to You as a sinner. Today, I am asking You to come and live in my heart. I repent of all my sins. I accept You today, Jesus. Thank You for giving me a new life and a new nature. Satan, sin, I don't serve you anymore. From this day forward, I will serve Jesus Christ. I make Jesus Christ my Lord and Savior. Amen.

Congratulations! You are now part of the family of God. You might say, "That was easy!" You're right! God made it that simple. I know you meant what you just prayed, so now, it's important that you do a few things. You need to tell someone that you've given your life to God, find a Bible-believing church, and read your Bible. Your life is about to change for the better.

Now, back to Noah. What would make a man believe so strongly that he could build something of that magnitude and stay at it for so long? I believe it was his relationship with God; his everyday walk with God; his trust in God.

Because Noah kept himself balanced in his relationship with God, he didn't have to wonder whether he heard from God or some other voice. For Christians to hear the voice of God, they must have their minds clear of the clutter going on around them. This requires balance in their mind. Noah was sure about what he heard and Who he heard it from. Noah is recorded as one of the heroes of the faith in the Bible (Hebrew 11:7) because of that faithfulness and obedience.

Noah walked with God by faith. There was nothing else for him to rely on. He didn't have anyone encouraging him. He wasn't given a team of people to assist him with building the ark. There was no building committee. Everything that God asked Noah to do, he did alone, and he did by faith. The Bible says, "The path we walk is charted by faith, not by what we see with our eyes" (2 Corinthians 5:7, Voice Bible). We as Christians should look at our lives from time to time and ask ourselves: Who am I walking with? What voice am I hearing? Am I conducting life's business after God's voice?

Job Believed God

As mentioned previously, Job was a man who lived perfectly before God because he was upright, feared God, and persistently avoided all evil (Job 1:1). Job was a prosperous man with many possessions and much wealth. In fact, he was the greatest of all people in the East (Job 1:3). History tells us that in the time of Job, there was no Bible for him to live by. However, God had made a covenant with him at some point.

Regardless, Job's faith and belief in God were tested. Satan suggested to God that Job would only remain faithful to Him as long as he was wealthy. So, God *allowed* Satan to test Job. Job lost everything he had, including his family and his animals. He lost every penny he had to his name. But through all that, Job never wavered or became unequally yoked with God (Job 1:22).

If that wasn't enough, God also allowed Satan to attack Job's health (Job 2:5). Just when you think it couldn't get any worse, Job's wife began to attack him and question his belief and trust in God. She told Job that he should curse God and die (Job 2:9). But Job still refused to put his covenant relationship with God in jeopardy by getting into doubt and unbelief. He spoke no evil words against God. He remained yoked with God. Nevertheless, Job stayed faithful to his belief in God. He stayed balanced in his faith and belief in the Lord's promises to him.

If all of that wasn't enough punishment, his friends also came to "comfort" him, but instead took that opportunity to tell Job the reasons why they thought all this had happened to him.

Now to the good part of the story: Because of Job's unwavering belief and faith, God restored back double the animals and blessed him with as many children as before. Job is a man that we can learn from. He kept true to his faith and belief in God, even amid all his sufferings. Job, like Noah and many others in the Bible, stayed balanced in their everyday walk with God, even when it wasn't convenient.

Let's revisit the story of the scales. Remember, your life is the scale, and the scale is balanced by how you live your life. As Christians, we should all live by the Word of God. The different men we discussed did just that. They balanced their everyday way of living with the Word of God, regardless of whether they read it from the Bible or whether it was spoken to them by God Himself. They refused to accept the yoke of sin. They did not allow the haters and naysayers to deter them from the plan God had for them. It's very important that we daily walk with God in a balanced way because any other way of living is a false balance in the eyes of God. With all the sin and corruption that was happening in the days of Noah and Job, I'm sure they easily could have found an easier and more convenient way to live. But they chose to believe and trust God instead.

So, as we talk about living a God-balanced lifestyle, we are putting the focus on living for Christ rather than focusing on ourselves or living as the world does. Living purely out our own desires or the world's way of living is unbalanced all around.

Unbalanced Christians Think They Know It All

At times, we all think that our way is better. After all, we know what's best for us! Don't we? There is some truth to this, but what about the things you don't know? There are elements of our lives that we don't know about; some things are hidden from us. 1 Corinthians says, "But we speak the wisdom of God in a mystery, even the hidden wisdom, which God ordained before the world unto our glory" (1

Corinthians 2:7). Just like the wisdom of God's redemptive plan for man was revealed by sending His Son to the Cross, He also only reveals certain things about our lives through the wisdom we gain from Him. That is why it's vitally important to stay balanced with Him. There are people, even some Christians, that I have talked to who claim to know everything about everything. There is nothing you can ask them about that they will claim they don't know.

The Bible has a name for these kinds of people. Scripture tells us, "The way of a fool is right in his own eyes: but he that hearkeneth unto counsel is wise" (Proverbs 12:15). This is a powerful verse, one that I think we can all embrace from time to time. It lets us know that we don't always have all the answers, and if we ever think we do, then we're fools. Make no mistake, I didn't call anyone a fool; it's in the Bible. These kinds of people can be dangerous, and they often don't realize that Satan wants to use them.

Saul, before his conversion to Christianity and before his name changed to Paul, thought that destroying the people of the church was the right thing to do (Acts 8:3). I'm sure Saul was hearing about Jesus and what the Christians were doing throughout the land and vowed to put a stop to it. So, he set out to destroy the Christians in any way he could. But as Saul continued his threats and slaughter of the Lord's disciples, he soon found out that what he thought was right in his own eyes was completely wrong. In persecuting Christians, he discovered that he was literally persecuting Jesus Himself (Acts 9:5). Saul, not yet a Christian, was seeing and hearing about the disciples of Jesus, the

51

Christians, and the spreading of the gospel, but, in his own eyes, he still somehow thought it was right to stop it.

Look at Judas. Judas Iscariot was the disciple who betrayed Jesus Christ. Some might ask, "If Jesus knew that the Judas would be the disciple that would break covenant with Him, why would He choose him as one of His disciples?" Jesus must have seen something special in Judas to call him to be one of His disciples. We know from the Bible that after Judas betrayed Jesus, he tried to return the money. When the priest refused to receive it, he went and hanged himself (Matthew 27:3-5).

What would make Judas believe that he was doing the right thing by selling Jesus out to His enemies? Was it the thirty pieces of silver or was it something else? It really doesn't matter because he was unbalanced either way. Jesus must have thought highly of him because Jesus made him His treasurer. Judas, unlike Saul (who later became Paul), spent time with Jesus. One would think that after spending all that time with Jesus, he would have known better than to try and pull one over on Him. But Judas thought that he knew what was best. He thought he had it all figured out, as most fools do. Judas had another spirit working inside him. He loved money more than he loved Jesus. His plan failed, and it cost him his life.

Simon Peter (also known as Peter) was another of Jesus' disciples who behaved in a way that he thought was right in his own eyes. Scripture tells us that Peter was the first disciple to be called by Jesus (Matthew 27:3-5), as well as the first one to be called an apostle (Mark 3:14-16). Simon Peter was probably the most powerful disciple of the Twelve. Scripture implies that he was the elected leader of the other disciples (Mark 1:36, Luke 22:32). It appears that Peter's personality was more powerful and commanding than the other disciples.

Peter was the disciple who was willing to walk on water at the command of Jesus (Matthew 14:28). He was the disciple who always asked Jesus the uncomfortable questions, like how often he should forgive (Matthew 18:21). He was one of the three disciples to witness Jesus raising a little girl raised from the dead (Mark 5:22-43; Luke 8:40-56). He was also one of three disciples who were present at the transfiguration of Jesus (Matthew 17:1-2) and was present in the garden of Gethsemane where Jesus sweated drops of blood before His capture (Matthew 26:36-37; Mark 14:32-33). Peter was summoned by Jesus to prepare for their last meal together (Luke 22:8). He was the disciple who confessed Jesus as the Son of the living God (Matthew 16:13-17). And after the death of Jesus, Peter was the first disciple to see Him when He had risen from the dead (Luke 24:28-34).

I hope you got a good picture of the type of disciple Simon Peter was and his close relationship with Jesus. Even though Peter was one of the inner-circle disciples, and even though he witnessed and participated in so many miraculous moments with Jesus, he still lost his balance as a faithful disciple. He was unbalanced in some ways. For instance, Peter confessed that he would never be offended by Jesus and would stick by His side no matter what happened. We know from Scripture that Peter did not keep his word and lost his balance in Jesus. When Peter promised not to be offended by Jesus or abandon Him, he never thought the time would come when he had to choose between Jesus and himself. In that instance, Peter turned out to be a double-minded, unstable disciple.

Peter, of all the disciples, should have known better than to open his mouth and speak words that he might have to eat later. Peter had been with Jesus from day one, yet he still thought that what he was doing was right in his own eyes. I guess one could say that Peter was a fool for doing what he did. But what Peter did was not a surprise to Jesus. Jesus knew what Peter was going to do before he did it (Matthew 26:31-35, Mark 14: 27-31). Unlike Judas Iscariot, Peter was offered a second chance and went on to proclaim the gospel. I am reminded of how easily we can fall if we don't keep ourselves balanced with the Word of God. I will leave you with two passages of Scripture:

> He writes the same way in all his letters, speaking in them of these matters. His letters contain some things that are hard to understand, which ignorant and unstable people distort, as they do the other Scriptures, to their own destruction. Therefore, dear friends, since you have been forewarned, be on your guard so that you may not be carried away by the error of the lawless and fall from your secure position.

18 But grow in the grace and knowledge of our Lord and Savior Jesus Christ. To him be glory both now and forever! Amen (2 Peter 3:16-18, New International Version).

The things that happened to those people are examples. They were written to be warnings for us. We live in the time that all those past histories were pointing to. 12 So anyone who thinks they are standing strong should be careful that they don't fall. 13 The only temptations that you have are the same temptations that all people have. But you can trust God. He will not let you be tempted more than you can bear. But when you are tempted, God will also give you a way to escape that temptation. Then you will be able to endure it (1 Corinthians 10:11-13, Easy-to-Read Version).

A Balanced Christian Knows How to Love His Neighbor

Having a neighbor who is difficult to communicate with is one of the worst things a homeowner can experience. I must say that I've been there a few times in my life. Even though you try your best and put your best foot forward to make peace with them, nothing seems to work. You might be thinking right now, "I don't even like my neighbor! Why would I try to make peace with them?" News flash! They're probably saying the same thing about you. Obtaining peace is important in all areas of our lives, even if the other party doesn't want peace too. Did you know that God has called Christians to be peacemakers? Matthew says, "Blessed are the peacemakers: for they shall be called the children of God" (Matthew 5:9).

A neighbor includes much more than just the person living next door to you. Your neighbor is anyone you might encounter. This especially applies to those of the household of faith (Galatians 6:10). Christians who are unbalanced in their walk with God use their words to destroy their neighbors. They pretend to be Christian, but their actions say otherwise. I'm not suggesting that just because you're a Christian that means you can't set things in order with your neighbor, if need be. But Christians who are always stirring up a mess are hypocrites in the purest form. They're dealing with a false balance, and their weight is unjust. They are frauds and imposters—false believers. Jesus warned us about these types of people. He said that counterfeit believers would be sown by Satan into the church to destroy it. Look at Matthew:

> He answered and said unto them, He that soweth the good seed is the Son of man; The field is the world; the good seed are the children of the kingdom; but the tares are the children of the wicked one; The enemy that sowed them is the devil; the harvest is the end of the world; and the reapers are the angels. As therefore the tares are gathered and burned in the fire; so shall it be in the end

of this world. The Son of man shall send forth his angels, and they shall gather out of his kingdom all things that offend, and them which do iniquity; And shall cast them into a furnace of fire: there shall be wailing and gnashing of teeth (Matthew 13:37-42).

Believers who are balanced in their way of living don't stir up trouble and spread rumors about others. This connects back to the tongue; when people are unbalanced and yoked with the devil, they not only destroy themselves, but sadly, they defile those who listen to the words their untamed tongue spurts out. I heard a great illustration from someone about gossiping: A gossiper usually knows where to take his garbage. Avoid making your ears someone else's garbage cans.

However, if you allow the weight of God's Word to tame your tongue, you can prevent yourself from falling victim to those who are out to slander others. You can break free from the verbal damage of those who are unbalanced in their speech through the knowledge of Scripture. Christians who are balanced in their speech and have allowed their tongue to be tamed by the weight of the Word of God will see right through those who try to destroy others with their tongues. The balanced person recognizes the damaging words as they hear them and casts them down (2 Corinthians 10:5). If unfruitful words do happen to fall on their ears but they are balanced in the Word of God, then they do not consent to or believe what they hear and will not repeat it. Look at this psalm:

Whoso privily slandereth his neighbour, him will I cut off: him that hath an high look and a proud heart will not I suffer (Psalm101:5).

I will destroy anyone who secretly tells lies about a neighbor. I can't stomach anyone who has proud eyes or an arrogant heart (Psalms 101:5, Common English Bible).

God speaks some strong words toward those who have an untamed tongue. The word "destroy" from the Oxford Language Dictionary simply means to put an end to the existence of something by damaging or attacking it. I'm not sure what God means by putting an end to those who sin against others with their tongue, but I don't want to be the one to find out what He means.

When people speak godly words and are in harmony with each other, communities and cities flourish with the blessings of God. On the other hand, communities are ruined and destroyed by people who have a wicked tongue and live by a false balance. Someone might ask, "Why is this the case?" Well, when you are balanced in the Word of God, you're a blessing to your neighborhood and community. Your godly influence and wisdom profit those around you, and because of your walk with God, the blessings on you are shared by those with whom you come in contact.

When Christians are unbalanced in their walk, talk, and living, they're a curse to the community they live in. Their speech is destructive, which will destroy unity and peace.

Unbalanced Christians are not looked upon favorably by others. When you stir up confusion and strife, no one wants to be around you. They rejoice when you are no longer around.

I like what this proverb says: "A brother offended is harder to be won than a strong city: and their contentions are like the bars of a castle. A man's belly shall be satisfied with the fruit of his mouth; and with the increase of his lips shall he be filled" (Proverbs 18:19-20). The wicked can destroy a city with their words, even if it has fortified walls.

People who tear down others are labeled by the Scriptures as lacking in wisdom, judgment, and understanding. Proverbs 17:28 says, "Even a fool, when he holdeth his peace, is counted wise: and he that shutteth his lips is esteemed a man of understanding." As a child, I can remember my mother saying these words to me when she thought I was talking too much: "Sometimes it is better to be seen and not heard."

A balanced person is a peaceful person. There is no peace without the Prince of Peace: Jesus Christ. The trouble with most unbalanced Christians is they want peace without the Prince. Peace in this world will come by no other means than having a balanced relationship with Jesus Christ. We must first be at peace with ourselves. Then, and only then, will we be able to have peace with others. Jesus said that He would give us peace that the world could not give us (John 16:33). Peace through Jesus only comes through having a balanced relationship with Him.

A Balanced Christian Walks in the Spirit

We have discussed the meaning of the word "balance." Now, let's talk about the word "unbalance." Unbalance would be the opposite of balance. But the word "unbalance" has other meanings. A few would be emotionally or mentally disturbed, deranged, troubled, unhinged, mixed up, mad, and off one's rocker. You get the picture. No love shown whatsoever. These are just a few definitions from the Oxford Language Dictionary. There is one definition in the Noah Webster 1828 American Dictionary of The English Language that really stands out to me: "not restrained by equal power." Let me explain.

According to these definitions, an unbalanced person is somewhat of a mentally ill person. I don't mean to suggest that if you ever find yourself unbalanced, you are suffering from some sort of mental illness. But a person who is unbalanced in spiritual things sometimes presents themselves as a person with some kind of mental problem. Nothing may be wrong with their brain, but in their mind, they are unbalanced. This is why we are told to renew our minds with the Word of God (Romans 12:2). By renewing our minds, we are brought back into balance with God.

Have you ever been in the shower, and you turned your head to one side so that the water from the shower could wash out your ear? If you do that for a long time, your equilibrium becomes off-balance, causing you to feel light-headed and unbalanced for a short time. I don't know how all that works, but things that were in balance are now unbalanced, causing your body to feel as though you have no control over it. Many people who have no history of mental illness exhibit signs of many of the meanings above. Most of them are so unbalanced in life that they are mad at the world. They don't know what it means to love or to walk in the spirit because there is a power restraining them, one that is unequal to the power of God.

If one meaning of unbalance is "not restrained by equal power," then balance would also mean "restrained by unequal power." The unbalanced Christian has two powers pulling against them: the power of the Spirit and the power of the flesh. Look what Galatians 5:17 says, "For the flesh lusteth against the Spirit, and the Spirit against the flesh: and these are contrary the one to the other: so that ye cannot do the things that ye would." The two powers are in a tug-of-war for control of your soul. This is the way the Bible tells us to walk in the Spirit, and the flesh will not have its way over us (Galatians 5:16). But I assure you that one will win over the other. There is no equal between your spirit and your flesh. Your spirit was made perfect at your new birth. But because we neglect the things of the Spirit, we make room at the table for Satan to come and dine. Satan is no match for the power of God. There is no equal between the two. The Spirit of God should be that *unequal* power controlling and ruling Christians' lives.

The unbalanced Christian is restrained by Satan and is used as his puppet to do as he pleases. Meanwhile, the balanced Christian is restrained by the Holy Spirit that lives inside them. Let the Spirit of God and His way of living be that unequal restraining power in your life. You will not be able to serve your flesh and your spirit. In Matthew, Jesus taught us how to keep from walking in the flesh. He said, "Thou shalt love the Lord thy God with all thy heart, and with all thy soul, and with all thy mind" (Matthew 22:37).

The Balanced Christian has a Spirit of Caleb

Most of us have probably read or at least heard of the story of Caleb and Joshua, along with ten others, who were sent to investigate the Promised Land. Most often, when this story is told, Caleb and Joshua are the two main characters talked about, and rightly so because they are the only two who returned with a different report.

But here I want to bring attention to only Caleb. You ask, "Why only Caleb?" Well, I'm glad you asked. Of the two men, Caleb and Joshua, Caleb is mentioned in Scripture as the one having another spirit with him. There was something about Caleb that stood out to God that Joshua didn't have. Both men released their faith and showed no fear when they saw the giants in the land (Numbers 14:6-9), but Caleb is the one in whom God saw a restraining power operating that was unequal to any other power—the power of the Spirit of God. Look at the following verses:

> Because all those men which have seen my glory, and my miracles, which I did in Egypt and in the wilderness, and have tempted me now these ten times, and have not hearkened to my voice; Surely they shall not see the

land which I sware unto their fathers, neither shall any of them that provoked me see it: But my servant Caleb, because he had another spirit with him, and hath followed me fully, him will I bring into the land whereinto he went; and his seed shall possess it (Numbers 14:22-24).

What was different about Caleb than Joshua? After all, Joshua spoke out to the people just as Caleb did! Why did God see something different in Caleb than He saw in Joshua? I'm not diminishing Joshua and his confession at all. He was a great warrior, who was chosen by God to be Moses' assistant and then later became his successor at his death. I suppose God could have said the same thing about Joshua that He did about Caleb. Joshua was Moses' right-hand man. But because Joshua was now to lead the people, he was looked upon by God as a leader and expected to act and talk like a leader.

Joshua was chosen to represent the tribe of Ephraim (Numbers 13:8) as they investigated the land. Joshua was already in a leadership position when they spied out on the land. The Bible says Caleb was sent as the representative of the tribe of Judah (Numbers 13:6). But Caleb is said to have had another spirit *with him* that none of the others had. Caleb did not show the spirit of unbelief and cowardice that the others did. This other spirit that Caleb had *with him* was the Spirit of God. Caleb had a spirit that was unequal to any other spirit in the other men. Caleb saw things the way that God had promised, and not as what his eyes saw—giants in the land. Caleb was balanced in this way of thinking because he believed that he could do exactly what God had said. He had another spirit controlling his flesh—the Spirit of God—not the spirit of the flesh.

The King James translation would indicate that this other spirit Caleb had with him was somehow accompanying him, as if walking alongside him. But the Jubilee translation records it this way: "But my slave Caleb, because there was another spirit in him, and he proved to follow after me, I will bring him into the land that he entered into, and his seed shall receive it by inheritance" (Numbers 14:24, Jubilee Bible 2000). Another spirit was inside Caleb: *another spirit in him.* This other spirit that Caleb was operating under was controlling him from the inside out. Sounds like the Spirit of God to me.

Caleb believed as God had said. Caleb spoke as God had spoken. Caleb's confession was the number one sign of another spirit controlling his actions and words. The other ten men had an opposite confession about what they saw in the land, and God called it evil (Numbers 14:37). Why were there different confessions when they all saw the same thing? It was because of the fear of what they saw in the land. As balanced Christians, we shouldn't have this type of spirit operating inside us. Caleb's confession with his mouth and his belief in his heart proved that he was being restrained by a spirit that was unequal to the spirit of fear. Never let it be said by God that your confession is evil. Greater He that is in us than he that is in the world (1 John 4:4).

Chapter IV
Balancing Our Material Wealth

Once again, I want to bring attention to Proverbs 11, which is God's warning to His children about living "yoked" with the world's way of living. The world has much to say about money and finances, very little of which is informed by the Word of God. So, another area where Christians can be unbalanced is in their finances. Wisdom is reflected in the way we manage our finances and in the way we deal with other people regarding money. Jesus frequently taught about the importance of faithfulness in our finances.

Many Christians cannot serve God in the way that they desire because their finances are unbalanced. They choose not to pay God His ten percent, the tithe, and are never able to give an offering. They don't give offerings because their way of thinking about money and giving is not reconciled with what God says about money. When we fail to honor God with our money, our lives become unstable and out of balance with the Word of God. This is just one of the results when we love money more than we love God.

Let us look at what God says about finances. In 1 Timothy 6:10, God said, "For the love of money is the root of all evil: which while some coveted after, they have erred from the faith, and pierced themselves through with many sorrows." Loving money more than loving God leads to self-destruction. Unbalance in giving God His tithe and giving offerings is robbing Him. When people love money, they become selfish in other things, not just their money. But as we see in 1 Timothy, it's the love of money that will get us in trouble. The Bible gives a great example of this:

> Will a man rob God? Yet ye have robbed me. But ye say, Wherein have we robbed thee? In tithes and offerings. Ye are cursed with a curse: for ye have robbed me, even this whole nation. Bring ye all the tithes into the storehouse, that there may be meat in mine house, and prove me now herewith, saith the Lord of hosts, if I will not open you the windows of heaven, and pour you out a blessing, that there shall not be room enough to receive it (Malachi 3:8-10).

So, we see from these verses that it is not a good thing to rob God. There are consequences when we choose to withhold what already belongs to Him. God loaned it to you for a little bit, but He does expect you to return it to Him. Someone might say, "It's all mine. I worked for it. Why do I have to give God a portion of it?" I have news for you. Nothing is yours. Everything you and I have in our possession belongs to God. He's the One that gave us the ability to work and make that money. He's the One that gave us that job. He's the One that provides the transportation for us to get back and forth from our job safely. Honoring God with your money requires a balance of the heart—the balance of putting God in first place when it comes to paying tithes.

God is not trying to withhold anything from us. To tell you the truth, He has already given us everything we need to live on this earth. The only thing God wants from us is our commitment to Him. He has committed Himself to us and everything we are involved in, and He is wanting that in return. All He is trying to do is get us in the position to receive from Him. Remember, the Word of God is your scale for weighing how you are to live. Don't get caught using a diverse weight when to comes to your money. Remember why you have money and how you got it. Look at Deuteronomy:

> But remember the Lord your God. For it is He Who is giving you power to become rich. By this He may keep His agreement which He promised to your fathers, as it is this day (Deuteronomy 8:18, New Life Version).

This is God speaking to the children of Israel after He had rescued them out of the land of Egypt. God promised them a land that we refer to as The Promised Land. This is the land that He promised to our fathers, Abraham, Isaac, and Jacob. This land has been *willed* to all those who will obey Him and keep His commandments. But let's look at the above verse in its full context:

> Be careful not to forget the Lord your God by not keeping all His Laws which I am telling you today. When you have eaten and are filled, and have built good houses to live in, and when your cattle and flocks become

many, and you get much silver and gold, and have many things for your own, be careful not to become proud. Do not forget the Lord your God Who brought you out of the land of Egypt, out of the house where you were servants. He led you through the big desert that brought fear with its poisonous snakes and scorpions and thirsty ground where there was no water. He brought you water out of hard rock. In the desert He fed you bread from heaven, which your fathers did not know about. He did this so you would not have pride and that He might test you. It was for your good in the end. Be careful not to say in your heart, 'My power and strong hand have made me rich.' But remember the Lord your God. For it is He Who is giving you power to become rich. By this He may keep His agreement which He promised to your fathers, as it is this day. If you ever forget the Lord your God and go to other gods to worship and work for them, I tell you today that you will be destroyed for sure. You will be destroyed like the nations the Lord destroys before you, because you would not listen to the voice of the Lord your God (Deuteronomy 8:11-20, New Life Version).

There is one more thing I want to point out in these verses. God gives a stern warning to the people. He reminds them to keep His laws and commandments and to remember where you came from and Who is responsible for it. Oh, how quickly we sometimes forget. It was God who brought you out of that mess you were in. It was God who healed you of that terminal disease. It was God who protected you when trouble was all around you. It was God who made a way when it seemed there was no way. Then it was God who gave us His most valuable creation—His only begotten Son, Jesus Christ. It is important that we as Christians don't forget these things and become unbalanced in our way of living.

An Unbalanced Christian will Rob God

For years I robbed God of His tithes and offerings. I was saved and loved the Lord, but I was unbalanced in Scripture and in my heart in tithing. The church I was saved in did not teach much about tithing, at least not that I can remember. What I do remember is the teaching on "paying dues." As I look back, I guess to them the tithes were what God was due. If that's true, then I certainly understand why they would think that. But teaching on paying tithes and that tithes belong to God and are holy—that I cannot recall. So, for many years, I was a non-tither. I was living with a false balance, and God did not approve of it.

Once I did begin to get revelation on paying tithes and how it could benefit me, I still didn't fully commit. For a long time, I dealt with the issue of the balance of my heart. I couldn't reconcile myself to the thought of giving back something that I was allowed to have in the first place. My reasoning was if God needed the tithes so badly, and if He is God, why doesn't He just get it and not allow me to have it in the first place? If it's that important to Him, why did He let me have it to begin with?

My first mistake was thinking that God needed my money. Man was I wrong! Why? Because it all belongs to Him. God doesn't need our money to remain God. The revelation I was missing was that God didn't want all my money. He didn't want the whole 100%, He just demanded a tenth of it. He wanted His tithe. All God asks of us is ten percent of the one hundred percent He has blessed us with. By giving Him the ten percent, you bless the ninety percent you get to keep. What a concept! Tithing is not the goal, it's the beginning to obedience to God, and it opens the windows of Heaven.

Consider the following verses:

> And he said unto them, Take heed, and beware of covetousness: for a man's life consisteth not in the abundance of the things which he possesseth (Luke 12:15).

> He that is faithful in that which is least is faithful also in much: and he that is unjust in the least is unjust also in much. If therefore ye have not been faithful in the unrighteous mammon, who will commit to your trust the true riches (Luke.16:10-11)?

When we withhold our tithes and offerings from God, we are covetous of what doesn't belong to us. If we have trouble paying the tenth, what other commands from God will we have a problem with?

The book of Acts 5 tells a story about a husband and wife, Ananias and Sapphira, who sold a piece of their property. They both agreed to withhold part of the money from the apostles, and something major happens because of their unbalanced way of thinking. Let's look at it from the Amplified Bible:

> Now a man named Ananias, with his wife Sapphira, sold a piece of property, and with his wife's full knowledge [and complicity] he kept back some of the proceeds, bringing only a [a]portion of it, and set it at the apostles' feet. But Peter said, "Ananias, why has Satan filled your heart to lie to the Holy Spirit and [secretly] keep back for yourself some of the proceeds [from the sale] of the land? As long as it remained [unsold], did it not remain your own [to do with as you pleased]? And after it was sold, was the money not under your control? Why is it that you have conceived this act [of hypocrisy and deceit] in your heart? You have not [simply] lied to people, but to God." And hearing these words, Ananias fell down suddenly and died; and great fear and awe gripped those who heard of it. And the young men [in the congregation] got up and wrapped up the body, and carried it out and

71

buried it. Now after an interval of about three hours his wife came in, not knowing what had happened. Peter asked her, "Tell me whether you sold your land for so much?" And she said, "Yes, for so much." Then Peter said to her, "How could you two have agreed together to put the Spirit of the Lord to the test? Look! The feet of those who have buried your husband are at the door, and they will carry you out also." And at once she fell down at his feet and died; and the young men came in and found her dead, and they carried her out and buried her beside her husband (Acts 5:1-10, Amplified Bible).

Now, I don't believe that God would strike you or me dead nowadays, at least not physically, for withholding a tithe or offering. But I do believe there are spiritual consequences when we lie and refuse to give to God what belongs to Him.

In this case, Ananias, and his wife Sapphira lied to God, and God was not happy about it. Remember, God only demands ten percent as a tithe; He never commanded that they give the full amount. The problem was that they lied about the amount it sold for to *appear* as if they had offered God the full amount. If they had told the truth about the money, we probably wouldn't be reading this story about them, at least not in this way. Ananias wanted the apostles to think that he had brought all the money from the sale of the land, and he got his wife to lie about it also. In today's world, we would call this "embezzlement." In simple terms, *they stole from*

God. It was in their power to do what was right. But because they loved money more than they loved God, they chose to lie and commit fraud against the God of Heaven. They were unbalanced in how they viewed money and operated with an unjust weight.

This is how Christians will conduct themselves when they are unbalanced in the things of God. When we hold back the part that God already said belongs to Him (Leviticus 27:30), the tithe, then we are essentially committing fraud against God. But we don't see it that way when we hold back the tithe or choose not to give offerings. How many of you would try something like Ananias and Sapphira did with the IRS? I don't know; you might. You would probably have second thoughts about it before you did, though. But we will do that same thing to God as quickly as we will take our next breath and think nothing about it. Yet all the time, we are spiritually killing ourselves.

Not only are there spiritual consequences, but I believe that robbing God also brings with it physical consequences as well. When we rob God in the form of the tithe and offering, we give the devil license to control our lives. This is not the balance, or the weight, God intended for His children to live by. When we cheat God, we are cheating ourselves out of all the promises of God. We work hard and can't seem to get ahead, always taking one step forward and two steps back. We keep from God what belongs to Him, we toil our whole life, and in the end, we have nothing to show for it.

God didn't save you so that you could spend your life yoked to the world's system. The world's system says, "Make all you can make, and keep all that you make. Steal what you can't make and lie about it to escape." We are the children of light, not darkness. God already knows what comes into your hands in the form of money. God wouldn't tell you to do something without giving you the means to do it.

When you say you can't afford to pay tithes, you are lying to God right then. You might say, "Well, I haven't lied to God about my money!" Maybe you haven't lied to Him about the *amount* of money you have, but you lied to Him when you said you couldn't afford to pay tithes. Why? If you work a job and receive money for it, you can afford to tithe because only 90% of it is yours. God declared that the first 10% of it is His. So having the job and receiving money for the work you do is the reason you can afford to pay tithes. The money you receive for working is the increase (Proverbs 3:9) that God commanded you to honor Him with. Look how the Amplified Bible records it:

> Honor the Lord with your wealth And with
> the first fruits of all your crops (income); I
> am thankful that God doesn't look at my past
> to determine my future
> (Proverbs 3:9, Amplified Bible).

Whatever you want to call it, increase, or income, you are commanded to pay tithes from both. Will a man rob God? Maybe the question should be, "Will *I* rob God?" The condition of our heart will determine how we use our money (Matthew 6:21).

Your quality of life is not based on quantity, but on quality. Your quality of life, all that you focus on, should be seeking first the kingdom of God and His righteousness (Matthew 6:33). Christians whose lives are balanced with the weight of God's Word will not rob God because they know that their tithing opens the windows of Heaven over their life and their offerings cause the blessings of God to flow out of those windows (Malachi 3:10).

Your life should not be about how much money and stuff you can acquire in your lifetime, but about living for God. God knows that we need things. But when things become more important than what God said was important, we are not living wisely. We are therefore living an unbalanced life. When we start to place a higher value on material things and a lesser value on how God desires for us to live, at that point, our quality of life starts to diminish.

When we stand before God, our wealth and material things will mean absolutely nothing, whether we got them honestly or dishonestly. It will not matter on that day. The only thing that will matter is where you will spend eternity. The Bible tells us that the things we have done on earth, our works, will follow us (Revelation 13:14). That is something to think about. Will you be labeled a robber of God in Heaven? Bible teacher J. Vernon McGee said, "Money will buy almost anything in this world, but it can buy nothing in the next world." A balanced Christian will not rob God.

The Benefits Outweighs the Sacrifice

Before I was all-in on paying tithes, not only did I try to reason with God about why I couldn't or shouldn't pay tithes, but I also told myself that I could not afford it. At this time in my life, I wouldn't consider myself as doing bad, but I wasn't doing so well in my finances either. I was what you would call hit-and-miss when it came to paying my tithes. I just couldn't bring myself to give my hard-earned money to the church. I know that many unbalanced Christians are thinking the same way. But one night I had an encounter with the Lord about money.

We miss out on God's bountiful blessings in our lives when we lack the faith to believe God in giving. Too often we lean on our own understanding rather than trusting God to do what He says He will do (Proverbs 3:5). Those who keep all that they gain have nothing more. But those who have generous spirits tap into the unlimited resources of God. Faith in God's Word makes the difference. If you truly desire to live a balanced lifestyle, you cannot exclude tithing as the first fruit of all your increase. Most people probably don't find themselves reading much from the book of Micah—at least I don't. But Micah shares some very interesting things. Let's look at a few verses:

> Do you expect me to overlook obscene wealth you've piled up by cheating and fraud? Do you think I'll tolerate shady deals and shifty scheming? I'm tired of the violent rich bullying their way with bluffs and lies.

I'm fed up. Beginning now, you're finished. You'll pay for your sins down to your last cent. No matter how much you get, it will never be enough—hollow stomachs, empty hearts.

No matter how hard you work, you'll have nothing to show for it—bankrupt lives, wasted souls. You'll plant grass but never get a lawn. You'll make jelly but never spread it on your bread. You'll press apples but never drink the cider. You have lived by the standards of your king, Omri, the decadent lifestyle of the family of Ahab. Because you've slavishly followed their fashions, I'm forcing you into bankruptcy. Your way of life will be laughed at, a tasteless joke. Your lives will be derided as futile and fake (Micah 6:10-16, Message Bible).

I wanted to share this passage of Scripture in its clearest context so that you would understand precisely what Micah is saying. Most of these verses, but not all, describe me at one time in my life. By some miracle, I never got to the point of filing for bankruptcy. I had a good job, making a decent wage, but had nothing to show for it. I was blowing my money on stuff that had no eternal value at all. It was all for my self-satisfaction and desire. I found myself living from paycheck to paycheck. For nearly two years I was living this way—just waiting for the next paycheck! I didn't know as much Scripture back then as I know today, so I was unaware of what God had done for me and made available to me. I was so unbalanced in His Word that I didn't know how to make things any different.

Then one day things got so bad that I had to decide to make some adjustments in my life. One of those adjustments was around tithing. I had to make what seemed like a huge sacrifice at the time to start paying tithes. The sacrifice of deciding to pay tithes turned out to be the biggest benefit of all time. That started over two decades ago, and I'm still reaping the benefits of it today. All because I got balanced with God in tithing.

Tithing is a Biblical principle. When Abraham received the revelation that God was and is the Possessor of Heaven and Earth, he paid tithes (Genesis 14:17-24). You may say, "This is Old Testament law." Look at these next verses from Hebrews:

> See how great he is! Abraham the patriarch gave him a tithe of the spoils. And those descendants of Levi who receive the priestly office have a commandment in the law to take tithes from the people, that is, from their brethren, though these also are descended from Abraham. But this man who has not their genealogy received tithes from Abraham and blessed him who had the promises (Hebrews 7:4-6, Revised Standard Version).

Tithing is just not an Old Testament law; it's a God-given law for all generations of people. Your pastor is required by God to take tithes from his congregation. The word "take" is a strong word when we are talking about the tithe. This is where many people misunderstand the whole concept of tithing. They think the church or pastor is taking their money. This is the way I thought for a long time. The pastor is just obeying God. He has a commandment from God to *take* tithes every time the doors of the church are open, and we have been given a commandment to *take* our tithes to the church or storehouse (Malachi 3:10). Our responsibility is to comply. We must be willing to freely give a tenth of our earnings when the pastor is ready to take it as the tithe. Remember, the tithe belongs to God and is holy unto Him (Leviticus 27:30), not the pastor.

You might say, "You mean if I go to church the pastor will take my money from me for my tithes?" No. So please, don't let this deter you from attending church. The priest or pastor is commanded to *take* your tithes only if you freely *give* them. Figuratively speaking, neither the pastor nor anyone else at the church is going to force you to give any amount of money to the church. We must be willing to give back to God what already belongs to Him (Leviticus 27:30). We are commanded by God to bring our tithes to the church (Malachi 3:10). When we refuse to do this, we are withholding a Holy thing.

This is how the Bible says that we should give: "Let each one give [thoughtfully and with purpose] just as he has decided in his heart, not grudgingly or under compulsion, for God loves a cheerful giver [and delights in the one whose heart is in his gift]" (2 Corinthians 9:7, Amplified Bible). If we give any other way, it would be out of balance with the way God says we are to give. Whatever we decide to give to the Lord's Kingdom, we must give from the heart and without strings attached.

Look at giving and tithing in this way: The church is the storehouse. The pastor is the manager or keeper of the storehouse. We are to *take* or *bring* our tithes to the church and offer them cheerfully and unbegrudgingly. Then, the pastor is commanded to "*take*," or a better word would be "*receive*," your money as tithes. This is not initiated by the pastor. Tithing starts with each person's willingness to give back to God what already belongs to Him and is Holy to Him. Doing it any other way is not tithing. If someone must force, guilt trip, or convince you to tithe, then it's not tithing, and you'll be better off keeping your money.

You cannot expect to go against the grain, do it your way, and yet still prosper in the things of God. You must do it God's way. You must choose to live by the scales of the Word of God and balance your way of living with what His Word says. I learned that being obedient to God's Word and paying God His tithes was more profitable to me than sacrificing all that I had worked so hard to achieve. I learned to do it His way and come into balance with His teachings.

The Unbalanced Christian will Become a Lover of Money

Let's look back at Deuteronomy 25:13-16 from the Message Bible. This is where Moses warned the people about using false balances and weights.

> Don't carry around with you two weights, one heavy and the other light, and don't keep two measures at hand, one large and the other small. Use only one weight, a true and honest weight, and one measure, a true and honest measure, so that you will live a long time on the land that God, your God, is giving you. Dishonest weights and measures are an abomination to God, your God—all this corruption in business deals (Deuteronomy 25:13-16, Message Bible).

These are the social laws that Moses gave to the people regarding how they were to treat each other. Moses knew that acquiring money by cheating their brothers or sisters was an abomination to God. To use a heavier or lighter weight on a scale for buying and selling merchandise to receive more money was hoarding, corrupt, and fraudulent. The Lord demanded an honest weight and a balanced scale (Deuteronomy 25:15).

We know that money is not the most important thing in our lives, or at least it shouldn't be, because desiring money too badly will bring sorrow to your life. I know this to be true because I have experienced it. My years of living from paycheck to paycheck and going from pawn shop to pawn shop, just so I could have money to supply my selfish needs and evil desires, brought me to a place in my life where money became the heartbeat of my soul. I breathed, ate, and slept money in my mind, and it got me nowhere but desiring to have more and to get it any way that I could. When you get to a point in your life when obtaining and having money becomes your driving force, it's time to put the brakes on. A person of balance in the Word of God will not desire to live obsessed and possessed by money.

I read a verse in the Bible that I thought would solve all my life's problems if I could just get my hands on enough money. But it turned out that my life got worse. "A feast is made for laughter, and wine maketh merry: but money answereth all things" (Ecclesiastes 10:19). Notice how it's worded: *but money answereth all things*. Well, I found this to be untrue. Now, you may say, "Wait just a minute; it's in the Bible, so it's got to be true." Yes, it's in the Bible, and yes, it's true. But the way it's worded in the King James Version can be a little misleading.

If this is true, then why are so many rich people miserable and lacking peace in their lives? If this is true, then why do so many people die of incurable diseases every day? If money answers all things, why not just buy your way out of being miserable? Why not just go down to the corner store and purchase peace, or buy the healing you need for your body? It's not that money will solve or answer all the problems you may encounter in life, but rather, that money is needed to do most things in life. Money is just a tool we

82

use to exchange goods. Money won't buy you happiness, nor will it buy you freedom from your problems. But money will give you *access* to many of those things.

Let me give you an example: A person commits a crime and goes to jail for it. Money can bail him out, but it won't buy his way out of the punishment for committing the crime. He broke the law, and there is no price tag on buying your way out of the consequences it brings. This translation of Ecclesiastes 10:19 is worded better: "People enjoy eating, and wine makes life happier. But money solves a lot of problems" (Easy-to-Read Version).

The phrase, *but money solves a lot of problems*, is something that we all can relate to. Money does solve a lot of our everyday life problems. Do you need food? Money will buy it. Do you want to take a vacation? Money will fund it. Do you want to go to school? Money will pay for it. See the difference between the two verses and how they are worded?

But if we go on living thinking that money will solve all of our lives' problems, we are dealing with a false balance and must find reconciliation with the Word of God. The only way we can break from believing and thinking that more money means less problems is to yoke up with Jesus Christ and do things His way. His way is better than having all the riches in the world. You can be free in Him and in all that He offers. Remember, your life is the scale, and on one side of the scale is how you are living, and on the other side of the scale is the Word of God. Your way of living and the

83

Word of God should balance out. Balance your life and way of living with Him. I want to leave you with this verse:

> For men who set their hearts on being wealthy expose themselves to temptation. They fall into one of the world's traps, and lay themselves open to all sorts of silly and wicked desires, which are quite capable of utterly ruining and destroying their souls. For loving money leads to all kinds of evil, and some men in the struggle to be rich have lost their faith and caused themselves untold agonies of mind (1 Timothy 6:10, J.B. Phillips New Testament).

Balanced Christians Trust God with Their Money

Trusting God with our money is what Christians are commanded to do. Remember, if we're honest, it belongs to Him in the first place. We are to trust God with our money in the same way we are to trust Him with our salvation. If we can't trust Him for our salvation, which He has given to us as a gift, then how in the world will we trust Him with our money when He has given us possession of it first? It's like giving a child candy, then asking for it back. You're probably not going to get it back. The same applies to unbalanced Christians. Once they have the money in their hands, they're most likely not going to trust anyone else with it, especially if they have no control over how it's used.

84

Much can be said about desiring to have plenty of money or wanting to be rich. As we said before, money is just a tool that we use to exchange items or services. Money has no value to us unless we exchange it for something we need or want. The real value of money is that it makes us all stewards of God. Since the money belongs to God, that would make us stewards over God's money. Christian stewardship is built upon the principle that all we possess belongs to God, and it's our responsibility to manage it in a way that is pleasing to Him. It is God who has blessed us with life and strength and allowed us to either earn or inherit what we have. Therefore, we are God's stewards or managers of all that we have. If we are faithful stewards of our finances, we will be trusted by the Lord with even greater responsibilities (Luke 16:10-11).

As genuine believers, we should have a sincere desire to help others and do right by each other.

We are not to take advantage of each other or allow others to take advantage of us. We should show the same mercy to others that we would want to be shown to us. In Scripture, the basis for being merciful is the fact that God has been merciful to us.

We should also practice godliness in every area of our lives, especially in our financial dealings. Many claiming to be believers hinder the cause and mission of Christ due to their unwise financial practices. Sadly, many people who do not know Christ are more honest than some who claim to follow Christ. We need to be diligent and determined about what

God put in our hands. This area is vital because the world is watching, and unbelievers rejoice when so-called Christians are unethical in their business affairs.

There is no question that God wants us to prosper, because He tells us He does all through the Scripture. Psalm 35:27 says, "Let them shout for joy, and be glad, that favour my righteous cause: yea, let them say continually, Let the Lord be magnified, which hath pleasure in the prosperity of his servant." Also in 3 John 2, He said, "Beloved, I wish above all things that thou mayest prosper and be in health, even as thy soul prospereth." You can find Scriptures like these throughout the Bible. So, if you were wondering if God was concerned about you prospering, you can put that to rest.

An important distinction I want you to notice is that the word "prosper" is used in both verses above, not the word "money." There *is* a difference between the two. Let me explain. God is not concerned about if you have a lot of money. He doesn't have a problem with it, but He's not concerned about it. His main desire is for us to prosper in all areas of our lives. For this to happen, it requires balance in Him—balance in His teachings and in following His commandments.

The word "prosper," from the Noah Webster 1828 American Dictionary of The English Language, means to favor; to render successful; to grow or increase; to thrive; to make gain. When God declared that He desired for you to prosper, He didn't just mean money. He wants you to prosper in *every* area of your life: your spiritual walk, your health, your job, your business (if you own one), your everyday life. God wants you to prosper in mind, body, and soul, not only in your wallet. The money is just a by-product of prospering in these other areas.

Vine's Complete Expository Dictionary gives this definition of prosper: to help on one's way. When God said He wished that we may prosper, according to this definition, He is saying that He wants to help us on our way wherever He leads us. He is not going to help us if we are heading the wrong way and are not in balance with His commandments and teachings. God has a way for us, and that way is Jesus Christ (John 14:6). We must be yoked with His way and not the world's ways.

We must come to the realization that God is our Source. When we walk in His way, He will provide the help we need while we are on our way to prosperity. When we learn to prosper in this way, we can be confident that we are doing it Jesus' way and not our way. I like what 3 John 2 says from this translation:

> My dear brother, I ask God that you may be all right in every way and that your body may be well. I know that your soul is all right (3 John 2, Worldwide English New Testament).

The statement *that you may be all right in every way*, does not suggest that we can choose our own way, or every way that the world presents. It's a statement signifying that as we walk the way of Jesus, the way that He shows us, then we'll be all right because He is there to prosper us in it. This is walking and living in balance with Him. "Who is the man who fears the Lord? Him will he instruct in the way that he should choose" (Psalms 25:12, English Standard Version).

Obtaining money or an abundance of it is not the goal. The goal should be to prosper at the hands of God in every way that He leads us on this earth. Hoarding our money brings sorrow to our lives. But when we let God prosper us, our lives will be filled with His joy—unspeakable joy (1 Peter 1:8).

Chapter V
Balanced Christians are Content Christians

Getting to a place of contentment in our lives can be more of a challenge for some than it is for others. I'm a witness to that. When I was younger, coming to a place where I felt content was difficult. When I use the word "content," I'm referring to a place of peace and satisfaction, not a place where we're satisfied with whatever turn our lives might take. You're not called to live a life of "take whatever comes your way." If we're on this earth, then God's plan for us is to grow and prosper in Him.

The word "content" from the Noah Webster 1828 American Dictionary of The English Language means to satisfy the mind; to make quiet, so as to stop complaint or opposition; to appease; to make easy in any situation. The goal of every Christian should be to get to that place in their life where they are satisfied in their mind without complaint or opposition to the thing that they have been blessed with. The quicker we start doing it God's way and put our way aside, the quicker we'll find that place of contentment. Some people will never find contentment because they're looking in the wrong place.

I understand that we can be content in one area of life but not in another. For example, one might be content with finances but not with work-related issues. That's part of life. No one's life will ever be at the place where they feel everything is where it should be. Life is all about adjusting and finding a place of peace with what God has blessed us with. When we find contentment in God, we have found that place in our lives where we aren't worried about tomorrow. Reflect on what Matthew says:

> No man can serve two masters: for either he will hate the one, and love the other; or else he will hold to the one, and despise the other. Ye cannot serve God and mammon. Therefore I say unto you, Take no thought for your life, what ye shall eat, or what ye shall drink; nor yet for your body, what ye shall put on. Is not the life more than meat, and the body than raiment? Behold the fowls of the air: for they sow not, neither do they reap, nor gather into barns; yet your heavenly Father feedeth them. Are ye not much better than they? (Matthew 6:24-26).

These verses let us know that we *can* find that place of contentment in our lives. We find that place in Jesus Christ. When we're content in the things of Jesus Christ, we're stable in believing and trusting what He said. When we're stable in Him, we're balanced with His way of teaching.

When God created Heaven and Earth, He did it in stages. Getting to a certain stage in our lives takes time. No one is born into this world and wakes up the next day having it all together. Most of us, when just starting out in life, tend to worry and agonize about the direction our lives will take.

Some people live their entire lives worrying about and chasing money and material things. They never seem to find that place in life where they put all worry and anxiety aside. A place of contentment is only found in God. We grow in stages, but there should come a time when we stop searching and start confessing.

After God created the light and saw that the light was good, He didn't stop His creation (Genesis 1:3-4). He continued His creation over the next five days. God was not content until all that He desired was created. And after six days of creation, the Bible says He rested on the seventh day (Genesis 2:1-3). God was content after He saw everything that He had created and declared it was very good; He was content in His creation (Genesis 1:31).

I suppose that God could have continued to create things, but He found a place in His creation where He decided it was good and very good. Likewise, we as Christians must discover and settle into a place of contentment in our lives. Some Christians will never find that place of contentment because they are looking in the wrong places. Some Christians chase after careers, while some chase after other people. Your contentment is not found in another person, a job, a bottle, or by any way other than in Jesus Christ. God will certainly use people and circumstances to help get us to that place of contentment. But even then, ultimately, the final decision comes down to us. Until you decide to stabilize things in your life, remove the clutter, and balance your way of living according to the Word of God, you will always be chasing after something that seems to have no end. People chase after contentment all the time and don't know how to find it or can't even recognize it when it shows up. Contentment comes from knowing and serving Jesus Christ.

The Bible has plenty to say about being content. Let's look at a few Scriptures:

> A little that a righteous man hath is better than the riches of many wicked (Psalms 37:16).

> Better is a little with righteousness than great revenues without right (Proverbs 16:8).

> Better is a dry morsel, and quietness therewith, than an house full of sacrifices with strife (Proverbs 17:1).

> Better is an handful with quietness, than both the hands full with travail and vexation of spirit (Ecclesiastes 4:6).

> The sleep of a labouring man is sweet, whether he eat little or much: but the abundance of the rich will not suffer him to sleep (Ecclesiastes 5:12).

> Better is the sight of the eyes than the wandering of the desire: this is also vanity and vexation of spirit (Ecclesiastes 6:9).

Let us not be desirous of vain glory, provoking one another, envying one another (Galatians 5:26).

And don't be wishing you were someplace else or with someone else. Where you are right now is God's place for you. Live and obey and love and believe right there. God, not your marital status, defines your life. Don't think I'm being harder on you than on the others. I give this same counsel in all the churches (1 Corinthians 7:17, Message Bible).

Not that I speak in respect of want: for I have learned, in whatsoever state I am, therewith to be content. I know both how to be abased, and I know how to abound: everywhere and in all things I am instructed both to be full and to be hungry, both to abound and to suffer need (Philippians 4:11-12).

But godliness with contentment is great gain. For we brought nothing into this world, and it is certain we can carry nothing out. And having food and raiment let us be therewith content (1 Timothy 6:6-8).

Let your conversation be without covetousness; and be content with such things as ye have: for he hath said, I will never leave thee, nor forsake thee (Hebrews 13:5).

The verses above reveal that the goal of life is finding that place of contentment. I know I shared a lot of verses, but I believe this is one of the main areas where people, especially some Christians, are unbalanced in the things of God. They think that just because God said they *can* have it means they *should* have it. Most of the time when we think this way, we're setting ourselves up for chasing after things that will eventually hurt. Just because God said you can have it doesn't mean it's good for you to have. We can't look at others and base our contentment on what they have versus what we don't have.

Being unbalanced leads to beings unstable. Unstableness leads to discontent. Discontentment leads to never knowing what it means to be fulfilled in Christ. We must find that place where we stop running and chasing after all our dreams and desires. Some dreams are just nightmares with a vain glory attached to them, and some desires are not from God but rather our own way of thinking. When God gives you a desire, He will give you the means to fulfill that desire. If you have the newest, biggest, and fastest gadgets without peace, love, and happiness, then you can keep them. I'd rather be content with what God has blessed me with. This is living a God-balanced life.

An Unbalanced Christian will Risk It All

Until we find that place of contentment for our lives in Jesus Christ, we'll risk the things we've been blessed with. When we aren't content, enough is never enough. We will always have the thought of getting more and more. There is nothing wrong with having plenty, but plenty without contentment is folly because we lack the sense to know when we reach that level of sufficiency. The only way we can reach a place of contentment in our lives is through the mirror of the Word of God. The Bible is a holy book that we have been graced with to model ourselves after. This is something we can't boast about doing ourselves. 2 Corinthians 3:5 says, "Not that we are sufficient of ourselves to think anything as of ourselves; but our sufficiency is of God."

Life itself can sometimes be risky. I believe there are times when the people of God must take risks to fulfill their purpose on Earth. But risk-taking for Christians should be different from risk-taking for someone who doesn't believe in God. These types of risk-takers are always living on the edge, so to speak. Everything they're offered or confronted with; they are on like white on cotton. They never take the time to research, ask questions, or seek any type of counsel before jumping in headfirst. This is especially true when it comes to money. Every deal that involves money is not always a good deal for you. Some deals should be left to other people.

Christians who are discontent with life will never see the place where they are content. They're always seeking that perfect spot. They have their health and strength. They have good-paying jobs. They attend a great church where they are fed the Word of God, and they have a family that loves them. But even blessed with all this, they still aren't content and continue to seek ways to gain more. Remember what Ecclesiastes 4:6 says, "Better is a handful with quietness, than both the hands full with travail and vexation of spirit." Sometimes more is not better. The unbalanced will risk it all for a dollar. More is not always better. Bigger is not always best.

Christians who are balanced in their walk with God take opportunities, not risks, that come their way, but only after much prayer and counsel. At least, that's the way we *should* do it. Some may call this risk-taking, but I disagree. Balanced people are Word-guided people. They don't always just move on a hunch, even though sometimes our intuition is correct. But when we aren't reconciled with God, even our own intuition can misguide us into making bad decisions or wrong choices. We all miss it at times. But when we start with God at the forefront and something does go wrong, He is there to lead and guide us back to a better path. Unlike the balanced Christian, the unbalanced Christian jumps in and out of bad choices and decisions like the sun rises every day.

Let me share a personal example. I had purchased several pieces of very expensive stereo equipment during one of my tours overseas. Every time I ran out of money, mostly between paydays, and couldn't support my habits, I would take a piece of that equipment to the pawnshop and pawn it for whatever amount of money I could get—any amount that would help support my hungry, thirsty, and sinful appetite. But it was never enough.

I would pawn anything in the house that I thought I could get money for. Talk about living on the edge! I was digging a deeper hole for myself. Because the pieces of stereo equipment were important to me, I never wanted to sell them, so I just settled for the exchange of the dollar on the equipment, plus the pawn fees. When payday came, I would go and get my stereo equipment from the pawnshop. Whatever amount I received for it, I would have to pay more to get it back. I was going deeper and deeper into debt. But I couldn't stop. I was dealing with an unbalanced heart issue. I loved money and what made me happy more than I loved God.

There came a point when I had all but one piece of my stereo equipment in the pawnshop at one time. I didn't know how or where I was going to get the money to get it all back on payday. So, what I did was find something else of value in the house and pawned it at a different pawn shop. I was a risk-taker. I never took into consideration that I might need money for something else more important, like a family emergency or a car repair. None of that crossed my mind. All I could think about was losing my stereo equipment and not having money to support my bad habits. I was risking it all.

It's no fun when there is more of the month left than there is money. I had no knowledge of saving or budgeting. The word "budget" often isn't mentioned in homes when it comes to managing money. At least it wasn't in my house. I relied on the pawnshop to get me out of any money trouble between paydays. This is a terrible way to live and try to provide for your family. All the things I did for self-pleasure were driving me further and further into debt. Yet for some reason, I was still willing to risk it all.

All this was happening while I had a wife and a small child at home. I knew I had to take care of my family. Otherwise, the military would be breathing down my throat. I kept food on the table and paid the bills on time, for the most part. I had several credit cards, but they were all maxed out from cash withdrawals, unnecessary purchases, and late payment fees. Yes, I was a mess. Any way I could obtain a dollar, I did it. Keep in mind I was saved at this point—but I sure didn't act like it. This pattern was putting my military career and my family relationships at risk. I knew I had to do something to stop it, but I didn't know what. I had no peace within my soul. I walked around all day wearing a mask, figuratively speaking. I was hiding the real me.

This went on for about five years, until I got orders to move to another military base. There were major changes in my family, but nothing had changed in my heart, so I saw myself going right back to that same old way of living. In my heart, I had a sincere desire to change, but I wasn't sure how to go about it. Then something happened to me that I wasn't expecting.

In 1993, I was assigned to a new duty station overseas. Because this was an overseas location, there were no pawn shops for me to run to when I needed emergency "fix-me" money. That really made me feel helpless. What was I going to do when I ran out of money and still had days left before payday rolled around again? I didn't know anyone to borrow a few dollars from. I needed a change and didn't know where to find it.

My wife Brenda and I were living off-base while waiting for on-base housing. We weren't attending a church, and I really had no intention of attending one at the time. We both were saved, but our lifestyle didn't show it. It was New Year's Eve night in 1993 when my whole life changed for the better. I was reading a book about finances and how people, especially Christians, should trust God with their money. The more I read, the more I wanted to read. The author was talking about paying tithes and giving offerings to finance the work of God. When I read that, I stopped reading, went into the bedroom, and told Brenda that we were going to find a church to attend.

Brenda and I started attending a church service on base that was held in the chapel. It wasn't your traditional military structured church service. It was the type of service we both were accustomed to. We didn't start paying tithes right away, but I could sense that something was happening. I was experiencing a change of heart about the whole tithing and offering dilemma. I could sense a reconciliation between me and the things of God taking place.

My biggest problem with tithing and offerings thing was *me*. I had to come clean with myself about my money mindset issue—the mere thought that I was giving my hard-earned money away to anyone. But that night, reading that book, I learned a different outlook. Like many people, I just didn't understand how I could give away ten percent of my earnings while keeping ninety percent, and that it would somehow benefit me in the long run. Then one day, I learned about these verses in the Bible:

> Be not deceived; God is not mocked: for whatsoever a man soweth, that shall he also reap. For he that soweth to his flesh shall of the flesh reap corruption; but he that soweth to the Spirit shall of the Spirit reap life everlasting. And let us not be weary in well doing: for in due season we shall reap, if we faint not (Galatians 6:7-9).

I was being deceived, and I was the one doing it, with the help of the devil. All this time I had been sowing to my flesh and reaping the "benefits" of it if you can even call it that. I can tell you that once we started faithfully tithing and giving offerings, our lives changed. What was the most noticeable was that our outlook on the future became brighter. We gained a new hope, or at least I did.

The Scripture says God is no respecter of persons (Romans 2:11). When it comes to tithe, He starts everyone at the same point—ten percent. But the beauty of it is that as He increases us, He trusts us to increase our tithes. As you make more, your tithe naturally grows with it. No matter what your income is, the tithe is ten percent. I guess God could have come up with another system, but He didn't. He could have said, "As your income increases, your percentage of tithe increases." But He didn't. God is showing us His balance here.

Christians who are balanced in the things of God will take only calculated risks, meaning they carefully consider the advantages and disadvantages of their actions, while unbelievers will take uncalculated risks. These types of risks usually have danger written all over them. It's like taking instructions from the devil. He only reveals the good parts but never shows us the outcome.

If you're reading this, and you can identify with what I am saying, you might want to check to see how balanced you are when it comes to your money. Do you have a lot of possessions and are still discontented? Are you chasing after things that always seem out of reach? Is there peace in your life? Are you robbing God by withholding His tithe and refusing to give offerings? Maybe you don't tithe at all or maybe you're a hit-and-miss tither who just can't see yourself giving up your hard-earned money. Let me assure you that there *is* a better way to live. Give to God what belongs to Him. Be content in what God has blessed you with, and if He desires for you to have more, He will open the door for it.

I will leave you with this quote: "Live with a purpose; you will invest your life in something, or you will throw it away on nothing." If you don't like where you are in life, do the things to change it. But at some point, you must find contentment with it.

A Balanced Christian is Fully Supplied

We all want our daily needs met and will do whatever we can to make sure they are. But God said that He would supply not some, but all, of our needs according to His riches in Christ Jesus (Philippians 4:19). If this is true, and it is, then do many Christians struggle getting their needs met? They know what God has said about it but they have a hard time bringing it to pass. What could possibly be the answer?

Let's remember the word "yoke" that we discussed earlier. We referenced the two oxen being yoked together, which makes them a match or balance for their workload. Then we talked about the warning God gave about yoking an ox and an ass together, which would create an imbalance in weight, size, and workload, and how there would be disharmony in their relationship. Now, we'll look at our imbalance with God, our refusal to reconcile with His teachings, and the problems it creates in our walk with Him.

If you still use checks to do financial transactions or pay bills, you're probably already aware of the importance of keeping the checkbook balanced. Making sure your checkbook is balanced on a regular basis is vitally important because you could be spending money that you don't have.

I can tell you from personal experience that this is not a good thing to do.

I didn't learn much about using a checkbook to conduct money transactions growing up. I didn't really hear much about checks and writing checks until after I joined the Army. It wasn't until basic training that I really learned about checks and the advantages and disadvantages of using them. I personally didn't have a checking account in my early days in the Army, but I know some who did.

Checking accounts can be very helpful if they are used correctly and kept up to date. Special attention must be given to balancing them so that the money you have in your account is equal to what you have recorded in your checkbook. If this isn't done with care, then it could result in an unbalanced checking account.

When a checking account is not balanced properly, one can make the mistake of writing bad checks. This happened to me only once during my early years in the military, and I haven't made that mistake since. For some reason, I was under the impression—and I wasn't the only one—that if I had blank checks, there was money in my account, which meant it was okay to write checks. Then one day, I received an envelope from the bank with a pink slip inside. It read, "Insufficient funds" and had an overdraft fee attached to it. There was not enough money in my checking account to cover the amount of the check I wrote, and I was being charged a penalty fee for it.

Back in the late 70s and the early 80s, the Army did not appreciate getting a letter from a bank telling them that a soldier had written a bad check. As a matter of fact, you could even be dishonorably discharged if it happened too many times. Plus, you had to make good on the check and the bounced check fees. It was just not a good situation to be in.

Now that we have discussed the words "balance" and "reconcile" in checkbook terms, let's look a little deeper and compare these to a Christian and God. Imagine you are the checkbook and God is the funds. When you look in your checkbook, what do you see? Do you see negative or positive funds? Remember, you're the checkbook and God is the money. What do you see when you look at yourself? Do you see God, or do you see something else? If God said that He would supply all our needs, then why don't we see funds when we look in our checkbook? Here's the answer: it's the same reason that we don't see God when we look at ourselves. Look what the book of 1 Corinthians says:

> For now we see through a glass, darkly; but then face to face: now I know in part; but then shall I know even as also I am known (1 Corinthians 13:12).

When we look in the Bible, we see just a little about who God is and what He is like, but one day, we will come face to face with Him. The Holy Bible is our mirror. It's the book we look in to see who God is and who we are. When you look in the Bible and what you read doesn't match who you

104

are or how you're living, then you and the Bible need to be reconciled. You must reconcile your way of living to what you see in the mirror of God's Word. It's not the other way around. We don't try to reconcile or balance the Word of God to our way of living. The Word of God will not change to meet our standards. We must change to meet Its standards. Our lives should be a mirror that reflects the image of Christ.

Just like when our checking account doesn't have enough money in it to cover the check we write, and we get a notification that there are insufficient funds, could it also be possible that the reason we feel insufficient at times is because we're not reconciled with God? Could it be that we need to realign our way of living with His way of living? If *all* your needs are not being supplied for your everyday living, I suggest it's time for reconciliation—a balance— with the One who has the supply: Jesus Christ.

Chapter VI
Balancing Our Dealings with Others

Let's not forget what the Word of God says about a false balance in Proverbs 11:1-3. He said it's an abomination to Him. In other words, He hates it. But He didn't stop there. He went on to say He loves and approves of a just weight. Because God is just, He despises dishonesty in business dealings.

In Old Testament times, with the absence of coinage, scales were used in most daily commercial transactions. To increase their profits, many merchants used two sets of stone weights to weigh goods. A lighter stone was placed on the scales when selling so that a lesser quantity was sold for the marked price, and a heavier stone was used when buying so that more was obtained for the same price. That demonstrates the contrast between a false balance versus a just weight and being yoked with Christ versus being yoked with the world. Remember again the harsh description of double-dealing: It is an abomination to the Lord. God hates all sin, but Scripture reveals that some sins are especially disgusting and offensive to Him. Dishonesty in business dealings is one of those sins.

Have you ever had someone try and swindle you out of your hard-earned money or out of something that was valuable or precious to you? How did it make you feel? You probably felt violated and betrayed, especially if it was a close friend or someone you knew. All the while you thought they were your friend or someone you could trust. Once you realize it, your first reaction might be to retaliate in some way. These types of people love money and material stuff more than they love you or God, and if they claim to be a Christian, they are an unbalanced Christian. Their heart is not balanced in the things of God. Their desire and love for money are greater than their desire and love for the people of God. I refer again to Proverbs, "Divers weights are an abomination unto the Lord, and a false balance is not good" (Proverbs 20:23).

The word "divers" from the Noah Webster 1828 American Dictionary of The English Language means different or various. This is the same thing that is being stated in Proverbs 11:1, which says, "A false balance is abomination to the Lord: but a just weight is his delight." We can also see the comparison to the type of behavior being played out by the merchants in Old Testament times to take advantage of the people during the selling and buying of goods. God said to not treat one person one way and another person a different way. He demands that we be balanced in our dealings with others when it comes to money and in other life situations. When we withhold money, for any reason, from someone who has rightfully earned it, it is stealing.

Our Heart and Desires

There have been times in my life when I went into a store and made a purchase; I exchanged money for merchandise. I had a demand; they had my supply. After choosing my purchase and making my way to the checkout register, the clerk rang me up and told me the amount. After making the transaction, I realized that the clerk had given me too much change. Now I have a choice: Do I make it right or do I walk out like nothing happened? The clerk made a mistake, not me. Am I going to capitalize on it? Or am I going to reveal the error and return the extra change? The call was mine. Remember, God said a diverse weight is an abomination and a false balance is not good (Proverbs 20:23). Also, your way of living should be weighed on the Word of God's scale. His weight and scale are not out of balance. If you weigh all your decisions and dealings by using the scale of God's Word, then when it comes to dealing with others, you will never cheat them.

Let's look at Proverbs again:

> God hates cheating in the marketplace; he loves it when business is aboveboard. The stuck-up fall flat on their faces, but down-to-earth people stand firm. The integrity of the honest keeps them on track; the deviousness of crooks brings them to ruin (Proverbs 11:1-3, Message Bible).

> The Lord expects you to be fair in every business deal, for he is the one who sets the standards for righteousness (Proverbs 16:11, The Passion Translation).

> The integrity of the honest keeps them on
> track; the deviousness of crooks brings them
> to ruin (Proverbs 11:3, Message Bible).

The verses above prove that when we cheat and are dishonest, we have no integrity and live a life that is off-track with God. This type of living will ruin our lives. This is living an unbalanced life. You have allowed yourself to be yoked to the world's way of living. This is the time a reconciliation needs to take place in your heart, so that you can reunite with God Almighty. When we looked at the book of Micah before, I didn't point out some important details about this Old Testament prophet, details that I believe help bring to light how our evil heart desires can destroy us and the people we influence.

The name Micah means *who is like the Lord*. He was an Old Testament prophet who we first read about in Judges 17-18. He worshiped false gods and led the people to practice idolatry. The Bible says he had a house of gods (Judges 17). Micah spoke harshly against those who claimed to be prophets of the Lord and used his position to lead the people of Judah to false hope. Micah then had a visitation from the Lord. The book of Micah is a book about God's judgment on the people, their restoration, and the plea for the people to repent. Let's look at Micah again:

> Are there yet the treasures of wickedness in
> the house of the wicked, and the scant
> measure that is abominable? Shall I count
> them pure with the wicked balances, and

with the bag of deceitful weights? For the rich men thereof are full of violence, and the inhabitants thereof have spoken lies, and their tongue is deceitful in their mouth. Therefore also will I make thee sick in smiting thee, in making thee desolate because of thy sins. Thou shalt eat, but not be satisfied; and thy casting down shall be in the midst of thee; and thou shalt take hold, but shalt not deliver; and that which thou deliverest will I give up to the sword. Thou shalt sow, but thou shalt not reap; thou shalt tread the olives, but thou shalt not anoint thee with oil; and sweet wine, but shalt not drink wine. For the statutes of Omri are kept, and all the works of the house of Ahab, and ye walk in their counsels; that I should make thee a desolation, and the inhabitants thereof an hissing: therefore ye shall bear the reproach of my people (Micah 6:10-16).

God witnessed the people's sins, and He demanded justice against them. God had a discourse with the people and commanded that they keep their part of the law that they had agreed to. God was not messing around. God is the Judge and Jury. The people were the ones on trial, and they had been found guilty of idolatry.

The people constructed an idolatrous stronghold by displaying the carved images that Micah had made inside the house of God. Nevertheless, they kept God in their thoughts, used His name, and even prayed to Him. But they were not worshipping the God of Heaven. They were worshiping a man-made god. Their heart's desires were unequally yoked with God's desire for them.

A Covenant of The Heart

Idolatry is a sin that destroys man, robs the true God of glory, and cuts people off from His help. The Lord will not compete with false gods. Christians don't have to bow down to a statue made of wood or a graven image to commit idolatry. If Christians look to anything other than God as their source of meaning, provision, deliverance, and fulfillment, then they are looking to an idol. Christians are to worship and serve the Creator, not the creation (Romans 1:25). In my case, it wasn't gravened or molten images, nor did I have teraphim in my house as Micah did. My gods were strong drink, partying, and the love of money. These were the gods that I was worshipping, not the God of Heaven.

All sinful desires are the fruit of wicked hearts, and all godly desires are the fruit of godly hearts. When we are unbalanced in the Word of God and continue to live sinfully, our outward actions will soon catch up with our inner character. Look at this verse in Proverbs:

> Whoever is steadfast in righteousness will live, but whoever pursues evil will die. Crooked minds are an abomination to the Lord, but those of blameless ways are his

111

delight. Be assured, the wicked will not go unpunished, but those who are righteous will escape (Proverbs 11:19-21, New Revised Standard Version).

Notice God's strong and contrasting emotions in this proverb. He hates hearts that are crooked—twisted and perverse—and unbalanced in their way of living, but He delights in those who are upright and living by the weight of His Word. Take notice of the link between the way people live and their hearts. The real contrast in the verse is between the wicked and the upright, but the heart and its byproducts directly correspond. People say and do things that are crooked and twisted because their hearts are crooked and twisted. Wicked people need to have their behavior reformed, but before this can happen, they need to have their hearts transformed.

Those who are blameless and righteous in their walk before God have had a change take place in their hearts. They have found out how to balance their life with the Word of God rather than a false balance. They have had a change from the sinful nature that pollutes people's desires to the godly nature that is pleasing and acceptable to the Lord. A heart change starts in the mind. Look at the Scriptures below:

> I beseech you therefore, brethren, by the mercies of God, that ye present your bodies a living sacrifice, holy, acceptable unto God, which is your reasonable service. And be not conformed to this world: but be ye

transformed by the renewing of your mind, that ye may prove what is that good, and acceptable, and perfect, will of God (Romans 12:1-2).

Therefore if any man be in Christ, he is a new creature: old things are passed away; behold, all things are become new. (2 Corinthians 5:17).

A new heart also will I give you, and a new spirit will I put within you: and I will take away the stony heart out of your flesh, and I will give you an heart of flesh (Ezekiel 36:26).

We must seek to renew our minds and seek after the things of God. The only way to restore our minds back to what they were like before sin came into the world is through the Word of God. When we maintain a balanced diet of God's Word, it will keep us balanced in our everyday living. It will cause us to deal with a just weight and not a false balance.

We must ask God to examine our hearts and prove us. Scripture says the things of life originate from our hearts (Proverbs 4:23). Unfortunately, many life decisions are made from our heads or feelings. Your feelings are different from your heart. Your feelings originate in your mind. People who make decisions like this are unbalanced in the things of God. But even when decisions are made from the heart, some can still turn out to be poor decisions. Good and righteous decisions are made from a heart that is in balance with the heart of God.

It's only those with a renewed mind and a pure heart who have a desire to do right. Those whose minds are unrenewed and living with a hard heart have wicked desires and are walking unbalanced.

Look at Proverbs once again: "A false balance is abomination to the Lord: but a just weight is his delight" (Proverbs 11:1). Let's compare a falsely balanced person and a person whose mind is not renewed. A falsely balanced person and an arrogant person both claim to be "weightier" than they really are. They claim to be more important and popular than anyone else. They claim to know more about any subject that might come up. According to them, *they've got it going on.*

This is the same concept that the merchants used when they wanted to cheat people during a sale or purchase. They would use a weighted stone when selling goods and use a lighter stone when buying goods. Every deal was to their advantage. They were dealing with a false balance and an unjust weight. People who are deceitful and corrupt in dealings with others are haughty people, and their hearts are nowhere close to God's. The arrogance in their hearts has boiled up and spilled over into their everyday affairs.

A New Covenant of the Heart

Jeremiah was an Old Testament prophet who God called before he was even born (Jeremiah 1:5). God was putting

His words in the mouth of Jeremiah, even though he shied away from his calling by telling God he was just a boy without the ability to speak (Jeremiah 1:9). That's just like some of us. God calls us to do something, and immediately, we start making excuses. Jeremiah would eventually accept his calling from God.

Jeremiah's mission from God was to preach His message to the sinful nation of Judah. His job was to tear down and rebuild (Jeremiah 1:10). He was to preach God's judgment upon the people. One of Jeremiah's main messages was about a new covenant between God and the people. A new covenant was necessary because the people were constantly breaking the old one. God spoke of a covenant of forgiveness and grace that would be written in the hearts of the people—a covenant that would never change or need to be updated; a covenant not written on stones but one written in the hearts of people. This would be an everlasting covenant. These words are prophesied by Jeremiah:

> But every one shall die for his own iniquity: every man that eateth the sour grape, his teeth shall be set on edge. Behold, the days come, saith the Lord, that I will make a new covenant with the house of Israel, and with the house of Judah: Not according to the covenant that I made with their fathers in the day that I took them by the hand to bring them out of the land of Egypt; which my covenant they brake, although I was an

husband unto them, saith the Lord (Jeremiah
31:30-32).

You may be wondering what this has to do with being
balanced in God. Well, the people were living a falsely
balanced life, and the Lord was about to correct that through
His prophet Jeremiah. Jeremiah was not too happy about
what God had called him to do and tried to talk his way out
of it. He told the Lord he couldn't speak, and he was just a
child. This sounds like someone who doesn't want anything
to do with what the Lord was telling him. At some point
during this dialogue between God and Jeremiah, Jeremiah
must have shown signs of fear because God had to tell him
not to be afraid and that He would be there to protect him
(Jeremiah 1:8).

I believe it took some time for Jeremiah to digest everything
that the Lord had said to him. Jeremiah, like many of us,
probably struggled with the fact of being commissioned by
the Lord to carry out such a task. I certainly would have. At
some point, Jeremiah had to come trust the Lord. What God
had told him was part of his reasoning for trusting the Lord
to fulfill the covenant: *I ordained thee a prophet unto the
nations; I am with thee to deliver thee; I have put my words
in thy mouth; I have this day set thee over the nations and
over the kingdoms.* This was a lot for Jeremiah to absorb in
just a short amount of time. Jeremiah needed to align his
thoughts with the Lord's thoughts. He needed to balance his
way of thinking with the Lord's way of thinking.

I suppose that Jeremiah could have refused to come into a covenant relationship with the Lord's commands. Of course, the Lord would just have found someone else to do His will. The reason we read this story about Jeremiah is simply because he chose to accept what God called him to do. Jeremiah first had to receive the new covenant within his heart before he could preach the message of the new covenant to the people. Jeremiah couldn't operate with a false balance and still be able participate in the Lord's plan to spread His message about the new covenant. Jeremiah had to accept his assignment by using a just weight. We find these verses recorded in Hebrews:

> Not according to the covenant that I made with their fathers in the day when I took them by the hand to lead them out of the land of Egypt; because they continued not in my covenant, and I regarded them not, saith the Lord. For this is the covenant that I will make with the house of Israel after those days, saith the Lord; I will put my laws into their mind, and write them in their hearts: and I will be to them a God, and they shall be to me a people: And they shall not teach every man his neighbour, and every man his brother, saying, Know the Lord: for all shall know me, from the least to the greatest (Hebrews 8:9-11).

I don't know about you, but I'm thankful that God cares enough about me to establish a covenant that will forever remain on my mind and in my heart. God saw that the old covenant was not good enough for you or me, so He created a new one, one that we could keep with us forever.

Chapter VII
Balancing Our Journey and Destination

We're all on a journey. This place called Earth is not our home; we're just passing through. One day, if Jesus tarries, we'll all complete our journey here and finally arrive at our destination, wherever that is. I hope your destination is Heaven.

While we're on Earth, we all have a different path. We'll experience different things, have different struggles and challenges, have different goals and dreams, and certainly have a different mission from God. But we're all on a journey.

Many people, especially Christians, go through the journey of their life missing out on what God has prepared for them because they're concentrated on the outcome. This is living an unbalanced life. Both the journey and the destination should be looked at as part of God's plan for us.

Other than marrying Brenda and being filled with the Holy Spirit with the evidence of speaking in other tongues, making Jesus Christ the Lord and Savior of my life is the most important decision I have ever made. The decisions I make while I am on this earth are important for living a balanced lifestyle, but of all the decisions a person makes, the most important one is the decision you make about your eternity. Only after you accept Jesus into your heart does the work of finding balance in the things of God come.

Heaven is my home! My destination! I must admit that I do sometimes think about what life will be like in Heaven. Jesus told us to be watchful and ready for His appearing. But I can't focus all my time and energy on Heaven, other than making sure I do everything I can to get ready and stay ready. I'm also called to enjoy the journey here on earth and be ready to face all the responsibilities that come with it. When we fail to accept and take on the responsibilities that living life brings, we are unbalanced and living life with an unjust weight. Look again at Proverbs: "A false balance is abomination to the Lord: but a just weight is his delight" (Proverbs 11:1).

As mentioned earlier, everyone is going through life as a multi-tasker. If we could clone ourselves, some of us would do it just to get everything done. There are many tasks that must be performed daily. Some are performed for others, but many are for our own benefit, and therefore, become our responsibility, not someone else's. Parents have the responsibility of taking care of their children. As a husband, I have responsibilities toward my wife and the home. One of those responsibilities is to love and protect her. I also have the responsibility of providing for her. I know that ultimately, God is her Provider. But as her husband, God has given me that responsibility too. As a Christian, I have responsibilities toward God and my brothers and sisters in Christ. Whatever God has blessed us with, we have a responsibility to take care of it, even if it belongs to someone else, and they're just letting us borrow it (1 Corinthians 4:2). If we don't take those responsibilities seriously, it could cost us more in the long haul. God has given each of us responsibilities in life. While yours might be different from mine, no one is excluded. I have mine, and you have yours.

If you currently own an automobile or have in the past, then you are probably familiar with the term "balancing tires." To keep our cars and trucks moving smoothly on the road, it's vitally important to regularly balance the tires. Owning an automobile is like owning a house; there are responsibilities to maintain it. Maintaining the correct tire balance on your car or truck is a responsibility of the owner that cannot be overlooked. This is not the responsibility of the person you bought the car from. Automotive mechanics was my specialty during my military career in the United States Army. So, what I'm telling you is not hearsay, but something I've experienced firsthand.

Maintaining proper tire balance serves to correct the weight of the vehicle imbalance on the tires and wheels. This will help to ensure the smoothest ride possible, lessen tire wear, which will increase the life of the tire, and decrease the strain on the drivetrain. Look at it as a tune-up for the tires and rims. When tires become out of balance, they create an unstable ride and will not roll smoothly, which causes unnecessary wear on them as well as other parts of the steering system.

Similarly, when people are unbalanced in their walk, they might wear down the sole of one shoe more than the other one. These are two great examples of our lives when we are out of balance with God and His teachings. When our way of living is not balanced with the Word of God, it becomes like the unbalanced tires. It causes us to live an unstable, roller-coaster lifestyle that will eventually wear us out prematurely.

Tire balancing requires that every tire is balanced to the exact same weight. If one tire weighs more or less than the other three, then you have an unbalanced drivetrain, and it affects the entire steering system. Every single tire and wheelset must be yoked together if the ride of the vehicle is to be as smooth as possible. When we own and drive a vehicle, it's our responsibility to keep the tires balanced if we desire a smooth ride on the highway and to prolong the life of the tires and other parts of the steering system. Likewise, it is every Christian responsibility to keep his or her life balanced by the weight of God's Word. Just like one unbalanced tire affects the whole system, one unbalanced area of our lives will eventually affect our whole life.

As a Christian, living a balanced lifestyle according to God's Word is the greatest responsibility charged to each of us. I truly believe that if we keep our way of living balanced to the Word of God, then all the other responsibilities we have will be completed in a smooth and timely manner. We won't wear out prematurely. Choosing any other way of living is a false balance.

God's Help is in the Balance

We need help along our journey to make it to our destination. At the church I grew up in, I remember a program that mainly involved the children called "Children's Day Program." Children's Day was dedicated to the children, and all the children in the church were expected to participate in some way or the other. It could be reciting a Bible verse, reading a spiritual poem, or even singing a song. The scariest part of the event was that you had to stand in front of the entire congregation and do this. Nothing could have been more frightening to me as a little boy of three or four years old.

As a small boy, I never told my parents that I didn't like Children's Day, or rather, that I didn't like participating. I, just like all the other children, was expected to perform in some way. I could have fought it or went along with it. Most of the time I fought it, but I lost every time. My parents, mostly my mother, were not going to let me get away with doing nothing.

One saying sticks in my mind that I remember nearly all the children reciting. It went something like this: "What are you looking at me for? I didn't come to stay; I just came to tell you today is Children's Day." I can remember thinking, "They know what day it is. Why do I have to remind them?" It didn't matter if every child in the church said the exact same thing, the parents could sit back and proudly declare that their child participated.

As I got a little older, my mother wanted me to memorize Psalm 23. My mother loved Psalm 23, so she thought it would be a good idea for me to stand and say it on Children's Day. You're probably wondering why I'm telling you this story. Here's why. As a child, I didn't have much control over what my parents wanted me to do. I could have fought the decision that my mother made, but when Children's Day came, I knew I would be standing in front of all those people doing or saying something. The question was not *what* I would be doing or saying, but *how* I chose to do it. I could do it my parents' way, or I could do it my way. My way was much harder. I learned to accept the fact that I would be participating in the Children's Day Program, no matter what I said or did. It was non-negotiable.

But there was a bright side—Mom was always there to help me through it. When she decided that I would participate in the Children's Day Program, she also decided that she was committed to helping me from start to finish. That made the whole process a lot easier, even though I still didn't want to do it. All the other parents helped their children too. I remember Mom squatting down at a distance from me where I could see her. She would smile and instruct me on what to say by moving her mouth as I tried to read her lips. I had to come to an agreement with my mother and balance my way of thinking with her plan to help me.

When you know someone has your back, it gives you the courage to step out and do what you are called to do. Sometimes I think many Christian folks forget that they have help to do the things God has called them to do. When we discover that help, it should become non-negotiable, whether we receive it or not. God is a present help in a time of need. Psalm 46:1 says, "God is our refuge and strength, a very present help in trouble."

God is not only our present help in a time of need, but He is also our future help in a time of need. Jehoshaphat received help when the armies were about to destroy him and the people. Moses and the children of Israel got help escaping Pharaoh and his army. Help was sent to Daniel when he was thrown into the lion's den. Shadrach, Meshach, and Abednego got help when they were placed inside the fiery furnace. Peter had help when he was thrown in jail for preaching God's Word; God sent an angel to free him. Paul and Silas were in jail because they refused to stop preaching, and after they started praising God, God used an earthquake to free them. And let's not forget about the Apostle Paul—God rescued him repeatedly. God will provide the same help for you and me if we will just stay in balance with Him and His Word.

After I realized I had the help of my mother, I got a renewed mind. Suddenly, I felt empowered. When we accept the whole of God's Word as our help, it gives us a renewed way of thinking that we didn't have before. My mother knew I needed the help and support, just as God knows we need His help and support in life. God is there to help us in our time of trouble and need.

When we are committed to living a balanced lifestyle, we can expect God's help when trouble comes our way. It's not a question of *if* we have trouble but rather *when*. The Bible is clear that while we are living on this earth, we will experience trouble. Jesus said in John,

Behold, the hour cometh, yea, is now come, that ye shall be scattered, every man to his own, and shall leave me alone: and yet I am not alone, because the Father is with me. These things I have spoken unto you, that in me ye might have peace. In the world ye shall have tribulation: but be of good cheer; I have overcome the world (John 16:32-33).

There is trouble everywhere in this world, but the person balanced in Christ has a get-out-of-trouble-card with Jesus Christ.

Trouble Comes to Us All, but God is There to Help

No one will live a trouble-free life. If you haven't had any trouble in your life thus far, all I can say is keep on living. No one is exempt from trouble, but if you are living your life with a true balance and a just weight, you can be of good cheer. The Bible says that in our time of trouble, the God of Heaven will be our refuge (Psalm 9:9). I find the following verses personally relatable:

The Lord hear thee in the day of trouble; the name of the God of Jacob defend thee; Send thee help from the sanctuary, and strengthen thee out of Zion; Remember all thy offerings, and accept thy burnt sacrifice; Selah. Grant thee according to thine own heart, and fulfil all thy counsel. We will rejoice in thy salvation, and in the name of our God we will set up our banners: the Lord fulfil all thy petitions. Now know I that the Lord saveth his anointed; he will hear him from his holy heaven with the saving strength of his right hand. Some trust in chariots, and some in horses: but we will remember the name of the Lord our God. They are brought down and fallen: but we are risen, and stand upright. Save, Lord: let the king hear us when we call (Psalm 20:1-9).

Many years ago, I was serving in the United States Army and was stationed overseas when my mother unexpectedly passed away. My wife Brenda and I had flown back to the United States for the funeral. Prior to going overseas, we had left our car with one of my sisters. On our very first night back on American soil, we were driving on a dark, country road, and our car broke down. We were stuck on the side of the road with nowhere to go and no way to contact anyone. It probably wouldn't have been too bad, except that it was around 1:30 AM, and it seemed as though we were the only car still on the road that night.

We had no cell phone and no protection with us except a flashlight I always kept in the trunk of the car. Imagine being stranded with your spouse or family on a country road late at night, no streetlights, and no traffic moving on it. How would that make you feel? And to top it off, you have no way to communicate with anyone for help. That would be enough to make anyone feel uneasy.

After trying to start the car several times with no success, I decided to get the flashlight and look under the hood. After I saw nothing indicating why the car had stopped, I closed the hood and got back inside the car with my wife. It seemed like we sat on the side of the road for an hour, but it was more like fifteen minutes. Once I realized there was nothing, I could do to get the car running again, I started to feel fear come upon me. After all, the whole time we had been sitting there, not one car had appeared in either direction. Then the thousand-dollar question came from Brenda: "What are you going to do?" Not what are *we* going to do, but what are *you* going to do? Now the pressure was on me to do something, but I just didn't know what to do. I couldn't ask my wife to walk on a dark road in the middle of the night with nothing to protect her. So, I decided that walking was not an option. It was at least five miles to a gas station. Plus, we didn't know if it would even be open that late at night. And to make things worse, we had two large pieces of luggage with us.

With no traffic, no streetlights, not one house in sight, and usure of my next move, we continued to sit in the car on the side of the road that dark, early morning. I knew we needed help I couldn't provide. So, I called out to Jesus. I said, "Jesus, You, got to send someone." Those were my exact words. Immediately after those words came out of my mouth, I looked in the rearview mirror and saw a light in the far distance. Then I heard these words in my spirit, "That's your ride." I looked over at Brenda and told her I saw a car coming and that I was going to flag it down. She looked at me like I had lost my mind and said, "You don't know those people." I replied, "That's our ride. Lock the doors when I get out."

I got my flashlight and got out of the car and started waving it back and forth. As the lights of the vehicle got closer, I could tell it was slowing down. After it had gotten even closer, I could tell it was a van. Then as it pulled alongside me, I saw the words on the side of the van. It was a church van. It stopped, and I slowly walked up to the passenger door. The window slowly rolled down about halfway, and I heard a woman's voice. I began to explain to her that our car had stopped running and asked for a ride to the nearest gas station so that I could make a phone call. She raised the window and said something to the driver, who was a man.

Here I am standing in the middle of nowhere, and my wife is locked inside a car, not knowing what's going on or what's being discussed. I couldn't imagine what was going through her mind. After all, she wasn't in favor of me stopping the vehicle to begin with. After the lady and the driver were done talking, she lowered her window and said that they would give us a ride into town. The driver got out of the van and walked around to the back, where I met him. I suppose at this point they had determined that I wasn't a threat to them. I thanked him and told him that we had two large suitcases in the trunk. He helped me get them and placed them in the back of the van. I then got Brenda out of the car and explained to her that these people had agreed to give us a ride into town.

We got into the van and found a seat in the back. As we entered, I noticed there were other people in the back that appeared to be asleep. The woman asked me what we were doing out on the road so late at night. I explained to her that I was in the Army, stationed overseas, and was back for my mother's funeral. She expressed her sorrow and asked my mother's name. When I told her my mother's name, she acted surprised and said, "What's her mother's name?" I told her my grandmother's name, and she turned around in her seat as if stunned by what she had heard. Well, to make a long story short, the people who stopped to help us were related to my grandmother.

I don't believe it was lucky or a coincidence that these people were relatives of mine on my grandmother's side. After all, we had both recently been baptized in the Holy Spirit. This was God's way of sending us help once I asked Him for it. I could have allowed fear to control me and stayed inside the car with my wife. All the time, I had hope that God was going to get us out of that situation. I just didn't know how He was going to do it. Hope is something Christians must hold on to if they want to stay balanced in the things of God. The Bible says, "Hope deferred maketh the heart sick: but when the desire cometh, it is a tree of life" (Proverbs 13:12).

We talked all the way to the next town as we rode along in that van. And when we arrived, another surprise happened. The woman refused to have the driver leave us at a gas station as I had requested. Even though it was out of their way, they drove us all the way to the front door of my sister's house and waited until we were inside before they left. On top of that, they wouldn't even accept anything for their time. God not only responded to my simple request for help, but He also gave us five-star Kingdom treatment. Imagine that. He did it that morning, and I believe He'll do it again—not just for me and Brenda, but also for you in your time of need.

From time to time, I think back on that dark, early morning and wonder if things would have turned out differently if I hadn't been balanced in the things of God. Someone might ask, "What would cause you to get out of the car not knowing who you were about to flag down?" That's a good question. To tell you the truth, it wasn't *me* wanting to do it, but rather my *spirit* leading me to do it. If it was left up to *me,* I would have sat there in the car with Brenda. What if I was just slightly unstable and double-minded in my belief and faith in God? Without a doubt, I probably wouldn't have heard the Lord so clearly telling me that was our ride. Surely, I wouldn't have gotten out of the car to flag down that van. But I *knew* that God was a present help in a time of need and that He was willing and able to help if I called upon Him. He is there for you when you need Him too.

Having a need for help isn't a bad thing. I'll leave you with this lesson. There were two men having a conversation about life. One of them said the devil was constantly invading his life. The other man replied, "I don't have any trouble from the devil." His friend looked at him and said, "You and the devil both must be running in the same direction." That's something for us to think about.

Balancing the Scriptures for Everyday Living

We have been talking about balancing the entire Word of God in our lives. But when application of Scripture is needed in a certain area, we must balance our focus and attention on those specific Scriptures. Let me give you an example. As I write this, it's football season. A football coach is responsible for designing plays for the team to execute. The football coach, at least one who is knowledgeable of the game, wouldn't draw up all running plays for the offense for the entire game. Nor would he call for every play to be a passing play. Coaching in this way would be unbalanced coaching. He would be calling plays that would result in an unbalanced offense. The same would go for the defense. Based on what the opposing team is doing, the decision could be to call for a passing or a running play. But both must be incorporated into the game, or at least be part of the playbook for the game, even though they may not ever run those plays. Coaching in this way would be balanced coaching. Coaches must have the flexibility to change plays when necessary.

Balancing the plays in this way doesn't necessarily mean that the number of passing plays must equal the number of running plays. That's not how the game is played. Nor do we balance God's Word in this way for our everyday living. Just like in football, where each down will bring a different play, our everyday living circumstances sometimes call for a different book of the Bible, a different verse, or a combination of both. And just like every play in football starts with a snap from the center, likewise, with Christians, all circumstances of life should start with prayer.

One good example of balancing the Scriptures for everyday living would be around healing. You wouldn't read or meditate on a chapter or verse in the Bible that discusses finances when you need healing in your body. Nor would you focus on Scriptures that address salvation when you need peace in your life. This would be a falsely balanced way of using Scripture. I will say this, salvation is the open door to peace. If you need healing, you will seek healing Scriptures. If you need deliverance, you will seek Scriptures on deliverance. You get the point.

Let me give you another example. Let's look at a verse in the book of James that most Christians have quoted at one time or another in their life. In the book of James, we find these words: "Submit yourselves therefore to God. Resist the devil, and he will flee from you" (James 4:7). When I hear other quote this verse, it usually sounds like this: "Resist the devil, and he will flee from you." And to be honest, I have quoted it this way before myself. That sounds good, but that is not what the whole verse says. If we speak it in this way, we are using the Word of God in an unbalanced way, and therefore, it will not work in getting rid of the devil.

Notice what it says you must do first: *Submit yourself to God.* There is an order we must use when we approach this verse for help in getting rid of the devil. You must first submit yourself to God, and then resist the devil. That is the order and the only way the devil will leave you alone. And it might take more than once. I've heard Christians leave out the first part of this verse and only quote the last half and thought to myself, "That devil is not going anywhere." They will say something like, "I resist you, devil, now you have to flee from me." Well, to tell you the truth, he doesn't have to flee.

What I believe would be more effective in making the devil flee would be to say, "I submit myself to God and resist you, devil. Now you must flee from me." This is a balanced way of decreeing this verse over your life because now you've followed the order of the Scripture and have made it personal to your situation. The goal is to say what God has said, not to say it the way we want. Saying it our way does not give us the full effect of what the Scripture says. That would be unbalanced use of Scripture and will not get us the results we hope for. The devil won't leave your circumstances when you're operating with a false balance concerning God's Word.

One of the devil's duties is to deceive Christians about what the Word of God says. Do you remember when Satan approached Eve about eating fruit in the garden? Let's take a look at it:

> Now the serpent was more subtil than any beast of the field which the Lord God had made. And he said unto the woman, Yea, hath God said, Ye shall not eat of every tree of the garden? And the woman said unto the

> serpent, We may eat of the fruit of the trees
> of the garden: But of the fruit of the tree
> which is in the midst of the garden, God hath
> said, Ye shall not eat of it, neither shall ye
> touch it, lest ye die (Genesis 3:1-3).

What Satan told Eve about what God had said was only partially true. Even though Eve was not yet in the garden, it still does not change what God did and didn't say. The first deception of the devil was to approach Eve, because he knew that Eve wasn't present when God gave that command to Adam. Second, God gave Adam only one restriction for the garden, which was *not to eat from the tree of the knowledge of good and evil; if they did, they would surely die.* Satan's deception was to imply to Eve that God had given them permission to eat from *all* the trees in the garden (Genesis 3:1). Third, Satan deceived Eve into believing that they would not die if they ate from all the trees in the garden (Genesis 3:4). And this is yet another deception of Satan, getting us to believe that sin has no consequences.

Even though Eve was correct about them being allowed to eat the fruit from the trees in the garden, she left out the part about not eating from the tree of the knowledge of good and evil. You can see what could happen when we omit part of what God has said or say something that He hasn't said. This is what God said about the trees in the garden:

> And the Lord God took the man, and put him
> into the garden of Eden to dress it and to keep
> it. And the Lord God commanded the man,

135

saying, Of every tree of the garden thou
mayest freely eat: But of the tree of the
knowledge of good and evil, thou shalt not
eat of it: for in the day that thou eatest thereof
thou shalt surely die (Genesis 2:16-17).

It's important that we as Christians balance the Word of God
with the weight it carries. A Christian's whole life should be
lived by what God has said. The devil is a master at
deception. One of his main goals is to get us confused about
what God has said and make us believe He said something
different.

If Satan is not successful at deceiving us, he will try to tempt
us. Remember when Jesus had returned from the wilderness
after fasting for forty days, and Satan approached Him? This
story is found in three of the four gospels: Matthew, Mark,
and Luke. We'll read it from Matthew:

Then was Jesus led up of the Spirit into the
wilderness to be tempted of the devil. And
when he had fasted forty days and forty
nights, he was afterward an hungred. And
when the tempter came to him, he said, If
thou be the Son of God, command that these
stones be made bread. But he answered and
said, It is written, Man shall not live by bread
alone, but by every word that proceedeth out
of the mouth of God. Then the devil taketh
him up into the holy city, and setteth him on
a pinnacle of the temple, And saith unto him,

If thou be the Son of God, cast thyself down: for it is written, He shall give his angels charge concerning thee: and in their hands they shall bear thee up, lest at any time thou dash thy foot against a stone. Jesus said unto him, It is written again, Thou shalt not tempt the Lord thy God. Again, the devil taketh him up into an exceeding high mountain, and sheweth him all the kingdoms of the world, and the glory of them; And saith unto him, All these things will I give thee, if thou wilt fall down and worship me. Then saith Jesus unto him, Get thee hence, Satan: for it is written, Thou shalt worship the Lord thy God, and him only shalt thou serve (Matthew 4:1-10).

When I read this story, I think of God setting Satan up. The Scripture says that Jesus was *led up by the Spirit.* This was not something that Jesus did on His own. God set Him up to be tempted by Satan. One might ask why God would put His Son, Jesus, in a position to be tempted by Satan, especially after He hadn't eaten for forty days. One can imagine that Jesus was physically weak from not eating. But God had a plan in mind.

God wanted to show Satan that He was his superior. God knew from the beginning, when He led Jesus into the wilderness, that Satan would shoot his best shots when Jesus was at His weakest. Jesus might have been physically weak, but He was strong spiritually. Every time Satan tempted

137

Him with something, Jesus would immediately fire back with the Word of God. Balanced Christians keep Satan in his rightful place, under our feet, by using the Word of God.

I believe this is why God allows Satan to tempt Christians, just like He allowed Satan to tempt Jesus and others, like Job. God wants to show Satan and prove to us that we have the victory over the works of Satan and that he has been defeated. I use the word "show" instead of "prove" because God has nothing to prove to Satan. When God raised Jesus from the dead that was all the proof that was needed for Satan. But God must prove to Christians that they have authority over Satan and his works. Look what it says in Luke:

> I've given you true authority. You can smash
> vipers and scorpions under your feet. You
> can walk all over the power of the enemy.
> You can't be harmed (Luke 10:19, The
> Voice Translation).

The next time Satan comes to tempt you, just put him in his place and send him running. Keep in mind that he is most likely to attack us at our weakest points in life. At a time when you think things can't get any worse, here comes Satan. Don't lose your focus, because this is probably a setup by God, for Satan. God wants you to show Satan that he has no power or authority over your life if you are a balanced Christian, knowing that if you submit yourself to God and resist Satan with His Word, then you will be victorious every time. This is so critical for Christians to understand to keep their walk with God balanced. If Satan fails at deceiving us, he will try to tempt us. A word of warning: Just because you put Satan in his place once doesn't mean he won't be back for a second or third time. Satan will keep coming back to tempt us. But there is One greater that lives inside us (1 John 4:4).

Another passage of Scripture that's worth looking at as we continue to discuss the importance of balancing the Word of God is found in Proverbs. "Trust in the Lord with all thine heart; and lean not unto thine own understanding. In all thy ways acknowledge him, and he shall direct thy paths" (Provers 3:5-6). Just like there's an order to James 4:7, these verses from Proverbs also have conditions attached to them. You must do the first part before the whole verse will work for you. We must first trust in the Lord with all our heart, not rely on our own understanding, and consult God in everything, and *then* He will show us the path to take. Any other approach is living unbalanced and is considered an unjust use of Scripture.

Trusting in the Lord as the verse says, can be hard for many Christians. But trusting Him with all our heart can be almost impossible. For example, sometimes we want to trust God for the small things, the things that don't take too much control from us—the things we can pull back on if they seem to be getting away from us. If we have most of the control over a situation, then we feel as though we have an ace in our pocket, so to speak. So, we'll "trust God"—until we think it's time for us to pull out the ace card. We don't want to fully surrender to God until it's totally out of our hands, and many times, even at this stage, we still don't want to fully surrender. This type of "trust" isn't trust at all. It's not trusting God with all our hearts.

Instead of trusting God with all our hearts from the very beginning as the verse instructs us to, we wait until we've exhausted all other means of control, somehow thinking all along that we're helping God. God doesn't need our help. That's why He told us to trust Him with all our hearts in the first place. If we only trust Him to do what we feel He can do and take the rest to do ourselves, then we're living by a false balance and using the Word of God as an unjust weight.

Our inclination is to trust God if it looks like things are going along just fine and not getting worse. But you must ask yourself, "Am I really, actually trusting *God*?" We all need to ask that question of ourselves from time to time. The verse says to trust in Him with all your heart. What part of your heart are you not trusting Him with? Is there a part you're relying on a friend to come through for you? Is there a part that says God might do that for someone else, but He will never do it for you? Maybe there's a part that's completely given up on God because you believe there is nothing that can be done?

The three conditions of Proverbs 3:5-6 are given in verses 5 and 6a. There is one promise in verse 6b. But look at the promise! The promise is guaranteed only if all the other conditions are met: *He will make our paths straight.* God gave Christians the key to walking in harmony and balance with Him. You might say, "Well, I'm not sure that He'll make my path straight even *if* I meet all of the conditions." Well, Scripture says God offers us *all* a future with a clear, straight path with nothing in our way. He told us that His Word would be a lamp wherever we walk and a light to keep us on the right path (Psalm 119:105). God wants to set your life on a path where you're sure about every step you take.

When we trust in the Lord with all our heart, lean not unto our own understanding, and in all our ways acknowledge him (Proverbs 3:5-6), then we are in balance with His Word. Trusting God this way requires total alignment with Him to make our paths straight. When we're out of alignment with His Word, then we're unstable in our walk with Him. When we're unstable in our walk with Him, it's just a matter of time before we lose our balance and fall to our own understanding.

Both James 4:7 and Proverbs 3:5-6 are often quoted incorrectly, incompletely, or without understanding by Christians. Now, let's look at the third one. Three is the number of completions, so let's look in Isaiah:

> If ye be willing and obedient, ye shall eat the
> good of the land (Isaiah 1:19).

Notice how the King James version words it, "willing and obedient." Now, let's look at it with a different translation:

> If ye will, and hear me, ye shall eat the goods
> of [the] earth. (If ye be willing, and obey me,

then ye shall eat the good things of the earth)
(Isaiah 1:19, Wycliffe Bible).

Judah and Jerusalem were called out by God for their rebellion against Him. They had refused to learn anything about God. They were so rebellious and corrupt that God compared them to Sodom and Gomorrah. God was so angry with them that He said He would no longer hear their prayers and would hide His eyes from them. Judah and Jerusalem's hands were full of blood, but in His mercy, God was willing to restore them if they would repent and turn back to Him. If they refused, they would die. Regardless, they wouldn't listen.

After reading Isaiah 1, I wonder if the people of Judah and Jerusalem expected to receive God's blessings when they refused to listen to Him. Did they think that they could continue to live that way without offending God? That God would somehow overlook their sin? Because God *is* a merciful God, He gave them an opportunity to make things right with Him. He gave them a set of conditions to reconcile and balance their way of doing things with Him. If they were willing to do something, He was willing to do something.

God offered them the chance, but it was their choice whether to accept it and make good on it. Then, and only then, would they be reconciled and put back in a balanced state with Him. Eating and having the good things of the earth depended on their willingness to hear, listen, and obey God. Anything less than that, and all deals were off the table. If they weren't willing to hear and listen to what the Lord was saying, then they couldn't eat the fruit of the earth or have the good things of the earth.

The people of Israel found out the hard way that the only way to get God back on their side was to balance and reconcile with Him. They had to obey and do the whole of God's Word. They couldn't just be willing to hear what He said, they also had to do what He said. We cannot reconcile with the God of Heaven by using our own false balance and unjust weight. It must be done His way.

This is the way Christians must live their life; we must be non-negotiable when it comes to obeying God's Word—the entire Word. Have you ever read a verse in the Bible that you wish you hadn't read? Now that you what the Bible says about a situation, you're obligated to do what it says. God didn't give us instructions about things He didn't care about or mean to fulfill. To tell you the truth, He has already brought all things to pass. He is now just waiting for us to follow His commandments so that we can receive all He has for us.

We must balance our entire life using the whole Bible. We can't pick and choose which Scriptures we do and don't like. The Word of God will not work for you like that. We are not supposed to take anything away from it, nor add anything to it. Picking and choosing what you like and what's more comfortable for you is a false balance. Remember, all of God's Word is there for a reason. We're meant to live by it, and it benefits us only when we choose to wholly follow it. It's there to make us better in every way (2 Timothy 3:16).

143

A Seat at The King's Table

Through His Word, God has given us everything we need to live. He has left nothing out. If you need to do it, He's there to help. If you're in trouble, He's there to deliver you. The Scriptures confirm this. Look at 2 Peter:

> According to his divine power [he] hath given unto us all things that pertain unto life and godliness, through the knowledge of him that hath called us to glory and virtue (2 Peter 1:3).

"All things" means all things. If you need it, God has already given it to you. Notice the qualifying condition though: It's through the knowledge of Him. This is how you get all things—through the knowledge of Him, which is found in His entire Word. Getting your needs met requires that balance. It requires being yoked with Jesus and His teachings. The Passion Translation says it like this:

Everything we could ever need for life and godliness has already been deposited in us by his divine power. For all this was lavished upon us through the rich experience of knowing him who has called us by name and invited us to come to him through a glorious manifestation of his goodness (2 Peter 1:13, Passion Translation).

Look at the first sentence of the verse: "Everything we could ever need for life and godliness has already been deposited in us by his divine power." Nothing is left out, and He has already placed it inside us. This is how we get from fear to faith, from poverty to plenty, from torment to peace, from sorrow to joy. What a good God!

I have memories from childhood of my family all sitting together at the table for supper. Some may call it dinner, but we would call it supper. Regardless, it was the last meal each day. My parents would try to have everyone eat at the same time, but sometimes, it wasn't possible for Dad to be there because of work-related issues.

Eating dinner together as a family was a common household practice back then. This was a family tradition in most homes. In our home, every person that was considered a member of our household had a certain seat at the table. Mom would prepare the meals and let everyone know when it was time to come to the table. The only time I was not allowed to join the others at the table was when I was being punished for something I had done wrong. If I got out of fellowship with Mom and Dad, then I wasn't allowed to eat at the table with the rest of the family. Because I got out of balance with my parents, I was no longer qualified to sit at the table, even though there was a seat assigned to me.

You might say, "Well, at least you got to eat." Yes, I got to eat, but I was taken away from the place of provision and from the fellowship of the family. They never denied me food, but I just wasn't allowed to eat at the table and enjoy the company of the family. Before I was allowed to return to the table, I had to reconcile myself to those I was in covenant with—my parents.

The prodigal son from Luke 15 had to reconcile himself back to his father too, after he realized that his chosen life wasn't working for him. It was never his father's decision that his son lived in such a way, but totally the son's choice, which the father honored. When we as Christians find ourselves away from the Father's table of blessings, it's never the fault of the Father; rather, it's because of our own decisions.

The son allowed himself to become unbalanced by refusing his father's standard of living, which caused him to live much further below the standards his father had provided. He lost his seat at his father's table because of his unwillingness to live equally in accordance with his father's rules. Just as the father welcomed his son back with open arms, our Heavenly Father welcomes His children back with open arms and puts them back in their rightful place at His table. Stay reconciled and balanced with God's way of living, and you will always eat at the Father's table.

When Christians have lost their balance in the things of God, they take themselves out of covenant with God. It's never God who breaks covenant with us; we break covenant with Him. When this happens, even though the table of all His blessings is prepared for us, we don't get to sit at it and dine until we reconcile our relationship with Him.

Even at our worst, God always has the table of all His blessings prepared and laid out for our enjoyment. The only time we don't get to sit at it is when our behavior towards Him has become unbalanced. because of our behavior toward Him. At those times, all we must do is bring ourselves back into balance with His Words and teachings.

Let's look at a story in 2 Samuel that demonstrates another concept of sitting at God's table:

> And David said, Is there yet any that is left of the house of Saul, that I may shew him kindness for Jonathan's sake? And there was of the house of Saul a servant whose name was Ziba. And when they had called him unto David, the king said unto him, Art thou Ziba? And he said, Thy servant is he. And the king said, Is there not yet any of the house of Saul, that I may shew the kindness of God unto him? And Ziba said unto the king, Jonathan hath yet a son, which is lame on his feet. And the king said unto him, Where is he? And Ziba said unto the king, Behold, he is in the house of Machir, the son of Ammiel, in Lodebar. Then king David sent, and fetched him out of the house of Machir, the son of Ammiel, from Lodebar. Now when Mephibosheth, the son of Jonathan, the son of Saul, was come unto David, he fell on his face, and did reverence. And David said, Mephibosheth. And he answered, Behold thy servant! And David said unto him, Fear not: for I will surely shew thee kindness for Jonathan thy father's sake, and will restore thee all the land of Saul thy father; and thou

147

shalt eat bread at my table continually (2
Samuel 9:1-7).

After the conflict between David and Saul was over, David
sought to find a way to honor Jonathan, who had helped him
escape the hands of Saul. David was looking for anyone in
Saul's family to honor. He was told about Mephibosheth,
which was Jonathan's son and Saul's grandson.
Mephibosheth was lame.

David sent for Mephibosheth and assured him that he meant
no harm toward him even though his grandfather, Saul, had
tried to harm David. But David didn't stop there. He offered
Mephibosheth a seat at his table for as long as he lived.
David did this to keep his promise to Mephibosheth's father,
Jonathan. Getting to sit at the table of King David meant a
lot to Mephibosheth, because he knew he had done nothing
to deserve it. If anything, David should be angry with him
and seeking to kill him because of Saul's betrayal. But it
meant more to David to sustain and support Mephibosheth
because of the covenant promise he had made to Jonathan.

As Christians, we're like Mephibosheth in some ways when
it comes to sitting at God's table. We have done nothing to
deserve a seat at the Master's table. As a matter of fact,
sometimes we do things that should disqualify us from
sitting at His table altogether. But because of the covenant
promise He has made to each of us who stay in balance and
harmony with Him, we're granted a seat at His table, even
though most of the time, we deserve to sit alone.
Mephibosheth knew that he was not worthy of David's

compassion toward him, and therefore, he shouldn't have been welcomed to his table. When you've been assigned a seat at God's table, don't disqualify yourself by being unwilling to stay balanced and yoked with God.

This scenario required both David's and Mephibosheth's cooperation. Both men had to be equally yoked together in their agreement to reconcile the issues there had been between David and Saul. Mephibosheth had to agree to meet with David, and David had to honor his promise to Jonathan. If either had refused, Mephibosheth would not have been granted a seat at David's table, and David would have broken his promise to Jonathan. I'm sure Mephibosheth looked at David with some unforgiveness in his heart and surely, David had second thoughts about showing kindness to a man whose grandfather attempted to kill him numerous times. I'm sure it was a balancing act for both because both had to reconcile their differences and come into harmony with each other.

Balance in Releasing Our Faith

James talks about a double-minded person, which we discussed earlier. Double-minded people are not only unstable or unbalanced in their ways, but they're also unbalanced in their faith. Our faith will only work when we exercise and use it. Stagnant faith is faith that is not released for the purpose of changing our situations.

I view failure to release one's faith as "one-dimensional faith." What I mean is that when we don't put our faith into action, there's no depth to it. The faith is there because God says it is (Romans 12:3), but it lies dormant until we release it. Not releasing your faith and expecting to receive from God is like yoking an ox and a mule together; it will not produce the outcome you desire. Not releasing your faith is a false balance.

Habakkuk 2:4 is a verse that most of us are familiar with. When Christians quote this verse, they only quote the last part of it most of the time: "...but the just shall live by his faith." However, the verse says more than just that:

> Behold, his soul which is lifted up is not
> upright in him: but the just shall live by his
> faith (Habakkuk 2:4).

This verse shares the truth that as justified people, we need not be afraid of the enemy that comes against us because God will protect us. Habakkuk was worried that his city would be next on the destroy list. God had to assure him that because he was a righteous man, a balanced man, he and his city would be spared; it was because of his faith. The word "faith" in that verse refers to being faithful and dependable. Because we have been made right with God through His son Jesus, we're to have faith in God and God can depend on us. When we walk in harmony with God and His Word, we don't have to be afraid because God has promised us safety.

Just like in Habakkuk's days, there is chaos going on all around us. You might be wondering and asking God if it will come to your house. Will you and your family be affected by all the evil and destruction you witness every day? Just like God assured Habakkuk, He assures us, "Because your life is balanced with my teachings, you have been justified by Me and need not worry." All you need to do is have faith in God. Release your faith, and watch God do the rest. When we live by the weight of God's Word and allow it to balance our way of living, we can rest assured that He will protect and keep us from trouble. Because you have been justified, you can live by releasing your faith in God.

Releasing your faith has a direct impact, not only on the vision that God has for your life, but also on the vision that *you* have for your life. The most important thing is how your faith is released. There must be a balance in releasing your faith. You cannot release your faith with the scales of your life favoring one side over the other. One part of your life can't be filled with faith words and quotes, and the other part be filled with doubt and unbelief. When releasing your faith, you must release it in every area of your life.

Our faith will not work if we don't believe it will. When and how you release your faith will depend on whether you have belief or doubt that it will work for you. Martin Luther once said, "Miracles take place not because they are performed but because they are believed." This is so true. We can't wait to see it before we believe it. This is not faith, at least not God-like faith.

Being balanced in faith looks like this:

> And they come unto him, bringing one sick of the palsy, which was borne of four. And when they could not come nigh unto him for the press, they uncovered the roof where he was: and when they had broken it up, they let down the bed wherein the sick of the palsy lay. When Jesus saw their faith, he said unto the sick of the palsy, Son, thy sins be forgiven thee (Mark 2:3-5).

This is faith being released with balance. Notice the unwavering faith being released in this verse. We don't know, because the Bible doesn't tell us, whose idea it was to lower this man down through the roof of the building. Nevertheless, it took the cooperation of all involved, and it really doesn't matter whose idea it was because Jesus took notice of *their* faith. Jesus wasn't concerned with whether the man with the palsy or the people lowering him down released the faith. Jesus saw faith being released, and that is what healed the man. When we release our faith, the same results will happen for us. Whatever we release our faith for is what we will get.

Also notice this portion of the verses above: *when Jesus saw their faith.* You might be saying, "Wow, I didn't know you could see faith." What Jesus saw were their actions. They believed in something, and therefore, they acted in a way to get it. This is faith in action. Scripture tells us that true faith will produce action (James 2:20), which is the type of faith that is balanced with what God has said. When we say what God has said, don't doubt in our heart, and then *do* something to lead us to the expected outcome, we'll get whatever we said (Mark 11:23). When we get it in our hearts that our faith will work when we work it, believing becomes second nature. We mentioned James earlier, but let's explore it again a little deeper:

> What doth it profit, my brethren, though a man say he hath faith, and have not works? Can faith save him? If a brother or sister be naked, and destitute of daily food, And one of you say unto them, Depart in peace, be ye warmed and filled; notwithstanding ye give them not those things which are needful to the body; what doth it profit? Even so faith, if it hath not works, is dead, being alone. Yea, a man may say, Thou hast faith, and I have works: shew me thy faith without thy works, and I will shew thee my faith by my works. Thou believest that there is one God; thou doest well: the devils also believe, and tremble. But wilt thou know, O vain man, that faith without works is dead? Was not Abraham our father justified by works, when he had offered Isaac his son upon the altar? Seest thou how faith wrought with his works, and by works was faith made perfect? (James 2:14-22).

Without going too deep into those verses, I want to share a little about James' intentions when writing this. Many Christians today have the notion that works can bring them

153

salvation. This is false, and James' intention was to shed some light onto this misconception of the church. The same faith that you and I must speak out of our mouth is the same faith that will bring a person salvation. Faith cannot save us; it's faith in His grace to save us. Scripture says,

> For by grace are ye saved through faith; and that not of yourselves: it is the gift of God: Not of works, lest any man should boast. For we are his workmanship, created in Christ Jesus unto good works, which God hath before ordained that we should walk in them (Ephesians 2:8-10).

This verse lets us know that faith alone cannot save us, just as faith without corresponding works is dead. Many Christians live with the idea that if they can do enough good deeds, that will be enough to usher them into Heaven. The Bible does not teach this. There is only one way to Heaven, and that is through Jesus Christ (John 14:6). If we think that our work or any other way will get us there, we are mistaken. So, to make this clear, we cannot be saved by grace alone, even though grace has been granted to us, but we are saved through our faith by the grace of God.

Furthermore, we cannot be saved by our work or good deeds. Neither you nor I can do enough, long enough to earn salvation. It's a gift from God through His grace. We must have faith to enter that grace and accept Jesus Christ as our Lord and Savior. The Bible says our works should follow our salvation, meaning that our salvation should produce works, not that we work to earn our salvation. Karl Barth said, "Grace must find expression in life; otherwise, it is not grace." God's grace was expressed to us through His Son, Jesus.

Likewise, when we release our faith, it should be evidenced by the works that follow it. Our faith will only work when we couple it with work. After we speak faith words out of our mouth and believe what we said, then we must do something to complement the words we have spoken. Just as James says, faith without works is dead. Thinking that our faith will work any other way is a false balance.

Let's look at an example of salvation by grace through faith. Romans 10:9 says, "That if thou shalt confess with thy mouth the Lord Jesus, and shalt believe in thine heart that God hath raised him from the dead, thou shalt be saved." The Bible is the best example of salvation by grace through faith. Confessing with the mouth and believing in the heart is the work that one must do to be saved. If there is no confession with the mouth or belief with the heart that God raised Jesus from the dead, then there is no salvation. Every person is a candidate for salvation by the grace that God has bestowed upon them, but they must confess it and believe in it.

Now, let's look at examples of faith accompanied by works. One great example would be the story I shared about the man stricken with palsy who was let down through the roof just to be near Jesus (Mark 2:3-5). This is Faith-in-Action 101. Suppose the man and those who carried the bed decided to stay outside and wait for his healing? That wouldn't have been faith in action. But because they put action with their faith and belief, he was healed.

Another example of faith in action would be the story of the woman with the issue of blood (Mark 25:34). This woman just didn't sit back and hope that she would be healed as Jesus passed through the city. No! First, she pressed through the crowd to touch Jesus' garment. That was her action. Second, she confessed to herself that if she could just touch His clothes, she would be healed. That was her faith talking. She worked her way through the crowd to touch Jesus' clothes, and she released her faith by saying it with her mouth. And she got her healing. Not only that, but Jesus made her whole and complete, lacking nothing.

These are just two of many examples in the Bible. We can see that faith without works is dead. Faith is a spiritual concept that comes from the heart, not from the mind, and it's released by our words and actions. Romans 10:8 says, "But what saith it? The word is nigh thee, even in thy mouth, and in thy heart: that is, the word of faith, which we preach." When faith comes out of our heart, and we speak it out of our mouth, it's faith that's balanced with the Word of God.

Chapter VIII

A Balanced Christian Believes the Church is a Necessity

Did you know that the word "church" is not mentioned anywhere in the Old Testament? The church is not a building, but a group of assembled believers who have chosen to follow Jesus Christ as their Lord and Savior. We know from the Bible that the church started in the New Testament on the Day of Pentecost (Acts 2:1-4). The church could not be formed until it had been bought completely with the blood of Jesus Christ (Ephesians 2:13). Therefore, the church was founded upon the death, resurrection, and ascension of Jesus Christ (Ephesians 1:15-23).

I'm a big believer in church attendance. I grew up going to church every Sunday, sometimes two or three times. My mother would make sure that we went to church. There was no negotiation. She made the rules, and we followed them. After all these years, I'm still a churchgoer. I must confess that after I was of age, there was a period in my life when I became a prodigal son, probably like many of you. Somewhere along the journey of life, I got off-balance and became yoked with the world's way of living. But thank God for a mother who showed me the value of being a regular church attendee. That's what brought me back from being a backslider to a churchgoer.

The Bible is clear about the importance of regularly attending church. Jesus, the Head of the church, was regular

157

in His church attendance. After all, immediately after Jesus had spent forty days fasting in the wilderness and then being tempted by Satan, He went to church. We'll pick up the story there:

> And Jesus returned in the power of the Spirit into Galilee: and there went out a fame of him through all the region round about. And he taught in their synagogues, being glorified of all. And he came to Nazareth, where he had been brought up: and, as his custom was, he went into the synagogue on the sabbath day, and stood up for to read. And there was delivered unto him the book of the prophet Esaias. And when he had opened the book, he found the place where it was written, The Spirit of the Lord is upon me, because he hath anointed me to preach the gospel to the poor; he hath sent me to heal the brokenhearted, to preach deliverance to the captives, and recovering of sight to the blind, to set at liberty them that are bruised, To preach the acceptable year of the Lord. And he closed the book, and he gave it again to the minister, and sat down. And the eyes of all them that were in the synagogue were fastened on him. And he began to say unto them, This day is this scripture fulfilled in your ears (Luke 4:14-21).

The word "church" is not mentioned in the verses above, but the word "synagogue" is. In Jesus' days, a synagogue is what we would call the church today. The word "synagogue" simply means a gathering of religious Jewish people for worship and study. Ever since the Day of Pentecost, when a group of Christ-believers comes together for worship and study of His Word, then they are considered the modern-day church. The body of Christ is the church.

So, in the verses above, we see Jesus returning to His hometown of Nazareth. He's likely in the same synagogue He attended as a child, because everyone there recognized Him as a man they knew, Joseph's son. Jesus had a habit of going to the synagogue to worship and fellowship with the people. But this day, He went there to preach to the people. Despite His life circumstances, Jesus remained balanced in His church attendance. You might say, "Well, brother, I'm not Jesus!" You certainly aren't and neither am I, but Paul did tell us in 1 Corinthians 11:1 to follow him as he follows Jesus. This means Christians are to imitate Christ by doing what He did and saying what He said. If Jesus was a regular churchgoer—and He was—then we as Christians are meant to be regular churchgoers too. We're told to follow His actions. If we choose to live any other way, it would be living using a false balance and an unjust weight. Look at what the Scriptures say:

> In response to all he has done for us, let us outdo each other in being helpful and kind to each other and in doing good. Let us not neglect our church meetings, as some people

do, but encourage and warn each other, especially now that the day of his coming back again is drawing near. If anyone sins deliberately by rejecting the Savior after knowing the truth of forgiveness, this sin is not covered by Christ's death; there is no way to get rid of it (Hebrews 10:24-26, Living Bible).

In the verses above, there are three areas of urging or encouragements related to church attendance. The first one is *outdoing each other in being helpful, kind, and doing good*. The second one is *not to abandon our church attendance*. The final one is *to stir up and alert each other in these last days that Jesus is coming soon*. We are commanded to do these three things when we assemble for worship services. The buildings we gather in are just places that God has provided for His people to come together in one accord and unity. We, the people, are the real church. That's why it took the shedding of Jesus' blood for the church to be established (Ephesians 2:13). Alone, you and I cannot be an effective church. We need each other to work together in harmony with Jesus.

There is a fourth area in Hebrews 10:26 that I want to point out. It warns of *falling away from your faith and not being able to find that rightful place in Christ again*. The warning is that there will be no more sacrifice for your sin, so don't lose your salvation. Of course, falling away for a time or a season is not an unpardonable sin. It simply means that the death and sacrifice of our Lord and Savior, Jesus Christ, will eventually lose its effect on a person that continues to willfully sin. These verses are written to Christians, those who have tasted the knowledge of the truth of God and His Word.

We all remember when the virus known as COVID-19 struck the world. Like many others in our country and across the world, our local church was shut down for a period. During the shutdown, the thing I missed the most was the opportunity to attend church and participate in corporate fellowship and worship with other believers. It was something I was accustomed to doing week after week after week, and suddenly, it was taken away from me. Church attendance had become a necessity for my way of living. When we start to lose or have lost our zeal for fellowship with other believers, we're starting to distance ourselves from Jesus and opening the door to yoking up with the world's way of living. I know some Christians don't see it this way. But if Jesus attended church regularly, what excuse do we have? A person balanced in the Word of God looks at the church as a necessity for their journey here on earth and as a must to get to their destination—Heaven.

Balanced Christians Plant Themselves

When I use the word "plant," I'm referring to stabilization, the process of making our lives more secure and balanced, becoming stable, balanced Christians. The word "plant" from Vine's Complete Expository Dictionary means to bring forth, spring up, and grow. All these meanings have taken place in my personal life since I planted myself in a local church. In the past twenty-five years, ever since I've been planted in my local church, I have seen spiritual growth in my life. God has raised me up and brought me forward in ways that I couldn't have imagined, all because I made the decision to plant myself in a local church.

Planting myself in a local church was challenging after 25 years in the Army. Once I rededicated my life to Christ, there was an urgency about me that wanted more. I was hungry and wanted to learn more about God and Jesus Christ. Because I moved from one base to another every three years or so, it was almost impossible to plant myself in a local church. Therefore, I had little to no stability in my spiritual life that could allow me to grow.

I'm not suggesting that people serving in the military are unstable or unspiritual, but I do believe that it can be difficult to find an opportunity to plant themselves in a local church. Because of that, it was hard for me to become balanced in the things of God. As it turns out, the Bible has much to say about planting and harvest. Let's see what Jesus taught about it:

> Jesus said, Verily, verily, I say unto you,
> Except a corn of wheat fall into the ground
> and die, it abideth alone: but if it dies, it
> bringeth forth much fruit (John 12:24).

A farmer wouldn't plant his crop one day and then expects the harvest from it the next day. Why? Because the seed hasn't had enough time in the ground to die. The seed must have time to germinate, meaning it must stay in the ground or remain planted long enough for it to die and spring up. The process of germination allows the seed to die, develop a root system, and show signs of life. If the seed is disrupted or removed from the ground before it's ready for growth, the life that was in the seed is now dead and all potential fruit from it could be lost. Our lives are similar. Christians must remain planted in a local church if they want to see spiritual fruit produced in their life. Christians will never be balanced in the things of God if they are going from church to church.

I know there are times when Christians must uproot themselves and their families to be planted in another local church. For instance, in my case, serving in the military meant I had to uproot my life every few years. It's hard to establish root support in a local church when you're subject to moving every two or three years. There can also be other legitimate reasons, such as career-related moves or family reasons. These are exceptions; church-hopping should never be common practice.

Let go back to John 12:24, which reads, "Jesus said, Verily, verily, I say unto you, Except a corn of wheat fall into the ground and die, it abideth alone: but if it dies, it bringeth forth much fruit." Jesus is illustrating that He will have to die so that many can be saved. As a former sharecropper's son, I can relate to a grain of wheat dying in the soil and producing much fruit. Through Jesus' death, we became His spiritual fruit. His death offers salvation and eternal life to whoever will believe in Him. We are the spiritual fruit of His death.

It's no different for us as believers. Until you become stable and balanced in the place God has called you to be planted, and until you dedicate your service to Him in that place, then you're abiding alone and will not die to yourself, resulting in no spiritual fruit in your life or anyone else's. We as Christians are not only called to produce spiritual fruit in our personal lives, but also to plant and water others' lives, that they may produce spiritual fruit too. Christians are to the local church what a seed is to the soil. Christians are the seed, and the local church is the ground. Christians, at least obedient Christians, are to plant themselves in a local church, to die to themselves and take up the cross of Jesus Christ, just like the apostle Paul said in Philippians: "For to me to live is Christ, and to die is gain" (Philippians 1:21).

There are Blessings in the Planting

A seed of any kind must remain in the ground until it dies; then, it sprouts out of the ground. Christians are no different from a seed. We must also remain planted in a local church until we learn how to control our flesh, because it will never totally die. There is a blessing in the death of our flesh. If there is no death in our flesh, then there is no blessing in our lives. This is recorded in Romans:

> Therefore, brethren, we are debtors, not to
> the flesh, to live after the flesh. For if ye live
> after the flesh, ye shall die: but if ye through

164

the Spirit do mortify the deeds of the body, ye shall live. For as many as are led by the Spirit of God, they are the sons of God (Romans 8:12-14).

In the verses above, Paul is underlining the importance of killing the works of the flesh. He uses the word "mortify" to explain this. Mortify is a word that means to embarrass, shame, or humiliate. Christians are to work to put their flesh to shame and embarrass it by killing it at every opportunity that it tries to act out. I have found this to be a daily task. The apostle Paul even confessed that dying daily to the flesh was necessary (1 Corinthians 15:31). Dying to our flesh can only be done through the Spirit of God. When we start to do this, we put ourselves in a position to receive the blessings of God. There are blessings in the planting. When we are planted in a local church, we become stable. When we become stable, we start to grow spiritually. When we start to grow spiritually, we begin to experience the many other blessings of God. This is in balance with God.

Christians who are planted in a local church are stable and balanced *in* the things of God and are blessed *with* the things of God, just like a plant when it's next to a body of water that has a continual flow. The Psalmist put it this way:

Blessed is the man that walketh not in the counsel of the ungodly, nor standeth in the way of sinners, nor sitteth in the seat of the scornful. But his delight is in the law of the Lord; and in his law doth he meditate day and night. And he shall be like a tree planted by the rivers of water, that bringeth forth his fruit in his season; his leaf also shall not wither; and whatsoever he doeth shall prosper (Psalms 1:1-3).

Any tree or plant that's in a place with a constant flow of water can expect to produce fruit at maximum yield because they have consistent nourishment. Likewise, these plants are less vulnerable to harsh weather than if they were planted elsewhere. The blessings of provision, nourishment, and growth lie in and depend on where the plant is rooted. The same goes for us. Christians' blessings are found in where they're planted—their local church.

Christians should be planted in a church where their blessing becomes a blessing to others. Plants do not produce fruit for themselves. The fruit is for the purpose of supplying a need that others might have. When the Psalmist says that the leaves will not wither, he doesn't mean that planting yourself in a local church will exempt you from experiencing times of need. What it means is that if you do have tough, unpleasant days, then you won't become consumed by them. When we take a licking and keep on ticking, we know that we're blessed.

I know without any doubt that since I have been planted in my local church, I have grown spiritually in ways that I can hardly believe. There is constant fruit in my life, to the point that I can be a blessing to others. Not to speak for my wife, Brenda, but I can also see the fruit of God's blessings in her life. I know this wouldn't have happened if we had chosen to live our lives any other way. Living a God-balanced life is the only way to live to experience the blessings of God.

Closing

In writing this book, I have used several Old Testament Scriptures to help support my message. After all, God said that we should take what we read in Old Testament as an example of how we should or should not live (2 Peter 2: 5-7). Furthermore, the entire Bible is there for us to gain knowledge pertinent to living our lives (2 Timothy 3:16).

Everyone is trying to find that place of balance in their life. Some people will stop at nothing to achieve a balanced way of living. Unfortunately, many are looking in the wrong places. Some people seek money, while others seek fame as a way of balance and stability for their life. Then there are those who seek balance and stability in other people. Other people can assist with bringing balance in our lives, but they aren't our source. In fact, they themselves often have problems with sustaining their own balance and stability as well.

In life, I have come to realize that I can learn from someone else's mistakes, or I can learn from my own mistakes. I much prefer the former. If I can learn from other people's mistakes, then I can likely avoid at least some of those same mistakes. Christians can prevent themselves from making a lot of the mistakes that the world's system would bring by keeping themselves balanced in the Word of God. Christians are to share the yoke of Christ-like living. We are to live a life of balance and to balance every aspect of our lives using the weight of the Word of God as our scale for how to live. I heard someone say, "You only become more of what you already are." This is a true statement, especially if you never try to change the things you don't like.

> Therefore, my beloved brethren, be ye sted-fast, unmoveable, always abounding in the work of the Lord, forasmuch as ye know that your labour is not in vain in the Lord (1 Corinthians 15:58).

> To keep our balance in the Word of God, we must remain firm, unwavering, and un-changeable during our times of trails and fix our minds and hearts on the Word of God (James 1:12).